MAKING IT
TO ADULTHOOD

MAKING IT TO ADULTHOOD

The Emerging Self

by ARTHUR J. De JONG

THE WESTMINSTER PRESS

Philadelphia

ISBN 0-664-24942-6

Library of Congress Catalog Card No. 75-172700

BOOK DESIGN BY
DOROTHY ALDEN SMITH

Published by The Westminster Press ®
Philadelphia, Pennsylvania

PRINTED IN THE UNITED STATES OF AMERICA

To my wife, Joyce
and
to my children
Mark, Beth, Paul, Ruth, and Richard

CONTENTS

INTRODUCTION

In my work on a college campus I have encountered many students who harbor suspicions and feelings that something quite serious may be wrong with them. I suspect that what I have found happening in college students is no less true of high school students. They feel that they may be abnormal in some way or another. Because they are afraid to bring these suspicions and fears out into the open, there is no way for them to handle these feelings constructively. Often these young people become depressed and anxious, are much less productive in their studies than they might be, and feel unwanted, ashamed, and guilty. The burden they carry secretly makes them shy away from social relationships and therefore experience loneliness. They live under a pall of self-doubt, if not self-accusation. What they do not know is that they share such feelings with many other young people. They are experiencing the *normal* problems of adolescence.

The purpose of the book is to provide young people with a resource that may help them handle middle and late adolescence and early adulthood constructively by describing the work and the normal problems associated with these stages as well as by offering them some positions to consider regarding some of the value decisions they must make. The book may speak to specific problems that an individual reader may have, or in a broader way provide him with a map of the territory he is traveling. If used by a group, the book may stimulate discussion on topics of mutual concern, encourage the process of sharing experiences, insights, and values. The book is offered on the assumption of insight therapy, that understanding encourages freedom and growth.

Though written primarily for young people between the ages of eighteen and twenty-two, the book may also prove helpful to adults who work with young people: parents, teachers, ministers, and counselors.

The book is written from the point of view of developmental psychology which focuses on the stages of growth in the human organism. Developmental psychologists refer to the "work" that should be accomplished at a given time as "phase-specific tasks." In the developmental framework the various ingredients that make up the human organism must take their place and play their role *at a specific time* if the individual is to become a well integrated and mature person. The unique way in which all ingredients come together has a great deal of influence over the character of the person.

The development of the individual is not capricious nor a matter of luck. There is a life principle that draws a person into wholesome existence. There is an inborn tendency to grow to maturity. Given reasonable conditions for growth, all the ingredients that form the organism grow into place at the right time and in the right proportion. Erik H. Erikson calls this the "epigenetic principle" and holds that "anything that grows has a *ground plan,* and . . . out of this ground plan, the parts arise, each having its *time* of special ascendancy, until all parts have arisen to form a functioning whole." [1]

It must be emphasized that there is a particular *time* when each stage should be handled. If handled then, that stage provides the necessary foundation for later stages. If not handled then, handling future stages will become more difficult, if not impossible. For example, a youngster who is able to accept the new ingredients in the organism at puberty will be prepared to handle the later stages in sexual maturation. On the contrary, a youngster who, at puberty, forms a defense against emerging sexual drives and emotions may well have a difficult time accepting sexuality and handling sexual drives and emotions later, if he should then entertain accepting these.

Even though there is a special time for each stage, it should be remembered that these stages are artificial constructs. Each stage is not so easily defined; it does not actually *begin* at its time of ascendancy in complete isolation from the other previous stages. On the contrary, each stage in some sense begins in the beginning. Each stage is a part of and depends upon previous growth, and each stage in some sense lasts a lifetime. The stages are an integral part of a larger ensemble.

Handling the stages is always a matter of degree. Each resolution is on a continuum between a more healthy and a less healthy solution. Erikson uses the phrase "a sense of" to convey the fact that each resolution is a matter of degree. If there is to be growth toward maturity, each resolution should be more on the positive side than on the negative side of the continuum. However, there will and should be an element of the negative. For example, there should be an element of distrust to counter trust in order to avoid naïveté.

Another important principle upon which this book is based is outlined by Robert E. Nixon. Nixon describes the growth process as *work*.[2] There is a tendency to think of the years of childhood and youth as carefree. If indeed they are carefree, they are not insignificant years. They are among the most important years of life because of the growth stages resident in these years and the implications of these stages for the long years of adulthood. Youth have work to do, the work of mastering the stages that they face in these years.

The two stages that are related to adolescence and early adulthood in Erikson's scheme are Identity versus Identity Diffusion and Intimacy versus Isolation.[3] It is around these two stages that the book is organized. The first chapter attempts to describe the foundation upon which the adolescent must build. The rest of the early chapters focus on the phase-specific tasks, problems, and value decisions of middle and late adolescence, i.e., on youth who are in their late teens, while the second half of the book focuses on the phase-specific tasks, problems, and value decisions of late adolescence and early adulthood, i.e., on youth who are in their early twenties.

1

FOUNDATIONS
OF IDENTITY

Every human being lives with a certain number of givens in his life such as the fact that, from conception, he is either male or female. He is not given an opportunity to choose which of the two he would rather be. If an adolescent understands the givens he brings with him to adolescence, he can approach the psychological work he faces without self-reproach. If, in addition to understanding these givens, he accepts them, he will be in a better position to work with them, perhaps modify them, or even rise above them in an act of freedom.

The purpose of this chapter is to discuss how personality is shaped in childhood. We hope that the youthful reader will gain an understanding of the many factors beyond his control, gain an appreciation of the complex work he has already completed, and obtain a map of where he is in the developmental process.

The Role of Heredity

Each person is guided in his development by hereditary factors. Young people should know that such things as body size, body shape, early or late maturation, color of hair and eyes, texture of hair, as well as certain diseases, such as diabetes, are controlled by heredity and are quite beyond the influence of the will. Researchers from both the natural and the behavioral sciences are producing evidence that the biochemical makeup that we inherit may be responsible not only for physical characteristics and disorders but also for emotional characteristics and disorders. Understanding heredity may help a person take a realistic attitude toward inherited factors, especially factors that are considered unfortunate. Arthur J. Jersild points out that if adolescents understand the hereditary factors operating in their lives, they may be spared from blaming themselves or being blamed by others for conditions over which they have little or no control. Persons with inborn physical handicaps may be spared painful self-reproach or guilt by understanding heredity.[4]

Physical Maturation

Adolescence is considered first and foremost a psychological phenomenon; however, adolescence builds on puberty and therefore has a physical foundation. In fact, the physical changes that erupt in puberty propel the person into adolescence. *What happens* in the form of physical growth and body chemistry and *how the adolescent feels* about these changes have a profound effect upon the adolescent.

The picture of the young person experiencing a sudden burst of growth and signs of sexual maturation may be misleading, as though puberty is quite unrelated to earlier life. For a year or two before puberty begins, the endocrine system of both boys and girls is at work preparing for puberty. Each person follows his own inner schedule, controlled by the central nervous system. When the endocrine system receives the signal, it produces hormones that evoke a broad spectrum of physiological and anatomical changes. Though the results may seem sporadic and unpredictable to the young person as well as to the observer, in most cases the system is under control and proceeding according to plan.

Each individual differs as to *when* puberty begins and the *pace* it follows. Changes may begin "early" or "late" and may proceed "slowly" or at a "rapid" pace. Youngsters who are unhappy with their pace should not blame themselves because the timing and pace are out of their control. When the time does arrive, the sex hormones and the growth hormones act in concert to produce the vast changes of puberty. The *average* linear growth in boys and girls is from two to three inches per year. Some boys have been known to grow four or more inches in a year. This growth generally takes place in girls at age ten to eleven and in boys at age fourteen to fifteen. However, it is *normal* to experience growth either earlier or later. On the average, girls reach puberty two years earlier than boys. Depending upon which criteria are used to describe puberty, girls usually reach puberty between the ages of ten and eleven, while boys usually reach puberty between the ages of twelve and sixteen.

The sequence of puberty is as follows:

Boys: a. beginning growth of the testes
       b. straight, pigmented pubic hair
       c. beginning enlargement of the penis
       d. early voice change
       e. first ejaculation
       f. kinky pubic hair
       g. age of maximum growth

    h. axillary hair
    i. marked voice changes
    j. development of beard.

Girls: a. initial enlargement of the breasts
    b. appearance of straight, pigmented pubic hair
    c. maximum physical growth
    d. appearance of kinky pubic hair
    e. menstruation
    f. growth of axillary hair.[5]

Along with bodily growth and sexual maturation there is an increase in energy which is linked with the accelerated instinctual forces. The increased energy is not automatically matched by increase in the thought process and control mechanisms. The adolescent is often observed in awkward and impulsive behavior. Body coordination has to be updated. The thought process and control mechanisms, though adequate for life before puberty was reached, also have to be updated. This updating takes some time. There is an indeterminate gap between the increase in energy and the ability to handle such energy smoothly and effectively. The high automobile accident rate among adolescents is, in part, accounted for by this gap. If most adolescents experience an increase in energy, some individuals experience *marked inadequacy of energy,* in part because of the major metabolic changes that take place. Others may experience inadequate energy because of the anxiety they experience with these changes in the body. Instead of increased energy, they may experience constant fatigue.

Though puberty is the gateway to adulthood and therefore a notable experience, it is not without its problems. A statement made by Arthur Jersild brings this point home: "Before these changes occur the adolescent *is* a child; after they have occurred the young person can *have* a child." [6] It is well known that the growth spurt and the change in body size and shape with the development of the secondary sex characteristics have a profound psychological effect upon the young person. Perhaps the least of these is the awkwardness which the growing person experiences and the lack of confidence and the embarrassment which this may cause.

The timing of the growth process has more effect than is sometimes realized. The girl who matures early will be bigger than her peers, whether boys or girls. While she is still young, she has to deal with the responsibility of menstruation and its implications of adult sexuality. She must do so at a time when her peers need not have such concern, and thus she may feel alienated from them. She may experience rejection or she may think that she is odd or abnormal. In addition, she may experience early conflict with her parents if she attempts to play out a social role commensurate with her physical maturity. If early maturation proves difficult to handle, she may develop an intellectual or ascetic defense against her new level of sexuality.

Likewise, late maturation may be a problem for other girls. A girl may experience rejection if she fails to develop at approximately the same time as her friends. She may feel odd, or wonder if there is something wrong with her. She may develop dislike for her body which seems to be letting her down. She may develop feelings of inferiority. She may feel alone if, because of her late maturation, she is left out of social functions.

The timing of maturation is also important to boys. Feelings of inadequacy can easily arise in a boy who experiences late maturation and may persist even after growth finally occurs. Boys sometimes sense concern and even disappointment on the part of their parents over their slow maturation, thus increasing their frustration and feelings of inadequacy. Parents may show reluctance in granting an acceptable level of independence to slow-maturing boys, thus adding insult to injury.

Though for some boys early maturation is welcome, other boys experience difficulty with early maturation. There is a tendency on the part of parents, teachers, school officials, and the public in general, to place responsibility on the shoulders of a large boy. If the public sees a large boy, they may assume that he plays football. If he does not, they may inquire why not. The assumption that is made about a boy who is large for his age is that he has also attained psychological maturity, an assumption that may not be true. When a large boy encounters such pressure, he may feel that he is not measuring up, that he is letting people down, that he is inadequate for life, and that he is a failure.

The timing of growth may affect young people in still other ways. With his ultimate size and shape unknown to him, the young person may experience anxiety, depression, or both. He may not be able to proceed with the psychological side of maturation if he is unsure of how he will ultimately look and feel. Adolescence may drag out for such a person. To know that one is changing, but not to know how or to what extent, may be unsettling. Such a feeling does not contribute to self-confidence.

Other young persons, particularly boys, may purposely attempt to keep adolescence "open," hoping for more physical growth. Parents of a short boy came to me concerned about the morbid adolescence that their son was having in comparison with an older sibling for whom the process of adolescence went smoothly. Their son had experienced other signs of maturation—change in voice, beard, etc.—but had experienced very little growth. It appeared to me that this boy was perplexed about his lack of growth and was attempting to stall the conclusion of growth. Finding the lack of size distressing, he was "holding out" for more.

Another dimension of puberty with which young people frequently experience difficulty is the development of the primary and secondary sexual characteristics. The education in sexuality that a young person received as well as the general attitude of the family toward sexuality will determine, in part, how well the young person handles puberty. How a girl feels about bodily functions in general and sexuality in particular will determine, to a great extent, how she handles the onset of menstruation and the development of her breasts. How a boy feels about such things as "wet dreams," beard, and his sexual thoughts, in part, depends upon the attitude with which he has been surrounded at home. It is quite common for young people to experience uneasiness and even guilt over sexual maturation.

One area on which boys focus a great deal of attention is the size of sex organs, their own and those of the opposite sex. While using a sex inventory in the housing units on campus as a part of a sex education program, I have found that men frequently show concern about size. They believe, quite erroneously, that size has something to do with virility and fertility. They are concerned with the size of their penis as well as with the size of the vagina and breasts of girls. Size in no way affects virility or fertility. If a boy believes that size "says something about the

man" and if he feels that his sexual organ lacks sufficient
size, he may develop feelings of inadequacy and inferiority.
Large boys and men are particularly vulnerable. In addition to the fact that size has nothing to do with a person's
masculinity or femininity, it should be noted that size is
determined genetically and by sex hormones, both outside the individual's control, and therefore he should not
blame himself regarding size.[7]

Two other problems associated with puberty and subsequent adolescence are acne and obesity. Both may affect
the way the person feels about himself. Acne is an affliction that is characteristic of adolescence. Because it is so
visible and because it affects such a strategic part of the
body, the face, it is difficult for many young people to
handle. Sometimes it is associated in the mind of the
adolescent with punishment for sexual thoughts and activity. Such an association is unfounded and unfortunate.
The person suffering from acne can take some comfort
in the fact that acne disappears as the person moves into
adulthood. It is a temporary affliction which, nevertheless,
causes a great deal of despair and self-contempt. Obesity
is not necessarily so closely associated with adolescence,
though it often accompanies puberty. It is the "babyish-
ness" associated with obesity that causes the person distress. Frequently it is outgrown.

What the adolescent thinks of his body has a great deal
to do with his self-concept. Self-esteem is often impaired
or enhanced by what a person feels concerning his body.
Because of the vast bodily changes that occur, adolescence
is a crucial time in the development of a self-concept.
The growth of the teen culture with its stereotyped
images and the mass media which spreads and uses such
images are causing even more emphasis to be placed upon

one's physical appearance. The adolescent makes comparisons between himself and his peers and takes such comparison very seriously.

The Role of Family and Society

The family plays a strategic role in the development of the individual. For the most part, the influence of the family happens quietly and subtly, in everyday contact, through what Morris Rosenberg describes as "casual conversations, small talk, the easy interchange of ideas, the sharing of minor enthusiasms." [8] It is the *family system,* i.e., the total interaction pattern between all the members of the family, from which the person develops his role, his attitudes, and his pattern of interaction with others.

The home presents a different world for each child, in spite of the fact that the child belongs to the same family, i.e., has the same parents and brothers and sisters. Each member of the family is given his unique role to play. Each child goes through his developmental stages at a different moment in the family's history. Each child experiences life from a different position in the family.

The family environment has a lot to do with the self-estimate that a growing child develops. What makes this shaping process especially hazardous is that it is not so much what others *actually* think of the person, but what *he thinks they think of him*. His self-concept is the result of "reflected appraisals" in which there is a great deal of room for exaggeration and distortion. The development of self-esteem will be treated more fully in Chapter 6.

The family is influential in determining the way the individual eventually relates to the outside world. First, the role that the youngster played in the family as a child is usually applied to the external world in later years. For instance, if the child developed in the family as a "helper" type, he will play some form of that role as an adult. Second, the way in which the child related to family members is basically reproduced in relationships with persons beyond the family in later years. Third, from the family, especially from his role and perspective in the family system, the child gains a picture or an impression of what the world is like. There is a tendency to live as if that estimate learned in childhood is true. Finally, though the individual may modify these somewhat in later life, he gains and tends to keep the values that he learned in his early family life.

In late childhood and preadolescent years, young people become sensitive about the appearance of their parents and the social and economic status of the family. This fact becomes influential in the interpersonal relationships within the family and between the youngster and persons outside the family. It also affects the development of self-esteem. If the family is respected by others, it encourages self-respect in the individual. He can reach out to other persons with pride and confidence.

If the family has a healthy influence on the child, it can also have a negative influence. He may become confused if his mother and father have conflicting identities in mind for him or give him conflicting roles to play in the family. A child can become the battleground where parents attempt to get at each other or control the family. He may be the scapegoat within the family. The responsibility for the family's continued, if unhappy, existence may be placed on him or he may bear the blame for the family's malfunction.

When children become for parents a compensatory device by which the parents make up for their own failure, the self-esteem of the child is jeopardized. When parents force an identity or force a role onto a young person, an identity or role that feels alien or that, for one reason or another, the youth cannot accept, he may suffer from shame. In exasperation, if not purposely, a parent may remind the child that the parent has done a great deal for him and that he owes the parent something in return. The adolescent in particular is quite aware of his financial dependence and it is only adding insult to injury if this happens. Feelings of inadequacy and shame may plague the youth.

Children may be of psychological value to parents. Allowing children to develop independence may pose a threat in the form of a loss of purpose to a parent, especially the mother, or a loss of companionship. Parents may deny their children the right to meet persons of the opposite sex, or they may deny their children the right to earn money. Parents may appeal to their children's sense of loyalty and gratitude. They may belittle them and undermine their confidence, or they may feign illness to control their children for their own purposes or needs.

The lack of clear sexual identities in parents can also have an adverse effect upon a child. A father who is never home, or a father who, in the eyes of his son, has an aura of perfection which the son feels he could never match, may leave the son little alternative but to identify with his mother. A mother who, out of her own insecurity, plays a dominant role in the family may become the figure with whom the son identifies. Or, the mother may be so penetrating with her presence that she emasculates her son. A mother who is bored with her role, who feels that her work as a homemaker is mundane and meaningless, will not provide her daughter with an attractive feminine image. Without clear sexual images with which to identify, to imitate, or with which to relate, children may experience difficulty in making their own sexual differentiation.

Society also plays an influential role in human development. In many respects it is the society which dictates the shape of human personality. The family does the shaping.

Each society has an "estimate of reality" or world view. In fact, a society usually has one major world view that tends to control the society, as well as one or more minority world views that are tolerated by the majority. At least until a child reaches adolescence, and perhaps not even then, he is unaware that his world view is merely an *estimate* of reality rather than *in fact* reality. Within a world view, customs develop, traditions form, ways of doing things solidify, attitudes and practices become entrenched, all of which makes the estimate appear to the holder, especially to a child, to be the way things *really* are. For example, a child may receive from his parents or community such views as: Hard work is of great value, The Caucasian race is superior, Tragedy is divine punishment, Might makes right, etc. The world view that a given society holds is passed on very subtly, almost automatically, because it is held in the form of assumptions. Each child within a society is very much the product of his society because he is schooled so subtly and yet so thoroughly in these assumptions.

Each society sets the boundaries of childhood, of adolescence, and of adulthood. These boundaries have to do with chronological age as well as with standards of performance that a person must meet before he is granted advanced status. Each society promotes a certain temperament among its people, certain broad characteristics such as gentleness or aggressiveness. Each society defines masculinity and femininity. Normal and abnormal behavior is established by society. Standards of economic and social status and success are set by society. And even though the family is influential in inculcating a value system, the society, especially a rapidly changing society, may dictate even in this area. A child or adolescent may turn to society's values, attitudes, and behavior patterns if they differ markedly from the ones held by his famliy. Even the nature and duties of the family are suggested by the society.

This combination of physical, family, and societal factors was operating in the life of a young girl with whom I worked over a period of years. She had deep feelings of inferiority and shame, and periodically became very depressed. She grew up in a minority neighborhood in which a great deal of emphasis was placed upon high academic performance. She had two older brothers who did well in school, whereas she lived on a precarious academic line. Success in school was a mark of prestige in her community and she felt that her parents expected her to succeed as much as her brothers as well as to keep up the family name. Several physical factors also contributed to her problems. Because of an imbalance in hormones, a condition later corrected, she had a great deal of facial hair at puberty. This contributed to her sense of shame. During much of her childhood and still in adolescence, she was obese. Finally, her brothers gave her the feeling that, *as a girl,* she was wrong or inferior. She saw her femininity as inferiority. All of this added up to a negative self-image, a poor performance in school, halting social relationships, and much internal pain.

The Psychological Work of Childhood

An individual is not merely an "accumulation" of hereditary and environmental factors. True, in infancy and early childhood, it appears that the individual does little more than respond automatically to instinctual forces and environmental conditions. Slowly, however, a "self" begins to take shape and begins to function. That self, as early as infancy and childhood, begins to play a mediating role with regard to hereditary and environmental factors. As the self grows in power, it begins to function as the executive of the organism. Though the individual is profoundly affected by hereditary and environmental factors, the self or the ego begins to choose, correlate, shape, decide, etc. In short, the ego begins to express a will and develop a set of values. We refer to this activity of the ego as *psychological work*. The psychological work that a child performs shapes the personality of the child. And the psychological work that he performs in childhood has a profound effect upon the subsequent development of the individual. In childhood, the individual lays the foundation on which he will have to build as an adolescent.

There is a particular work assignment that needs to be accomplished at each stage, and the relative success or failure of each stage affects the succeeding stages, even if the work to be accomplished in those later stages differs. Erik Erikson describes the work of childhood and the implications for later life which result from the level of accomplishment reached in each stage.

The first task of the child is to develop a sense of *basic trust*. The negative alternative is to acquire a sense of *basic mistrust*. Basic trust is feeling an "inner goodness."

The child gains either trust or mistrust from his relationship with the mothering one. The child will internalize the trustworthiness of the relationship. The child will learn that he can count on her and can count on life. He will "conclude" that he can live assured that life is trustworthy. The "virtue" that arises in the child as a result of a good relationship with the mothering one is *hope*. If hope is acquired in childhood, it allows for and contributes to more advanced sets of hopes. Hope thus gains power and becomes a force in the individual's life.

The second task of childhood is to acquire a sense of *autonomy*. Autonomy refers to that condition when, on the one hand, a child gains personal control over some of the forces that affect his life, and when, on the other hand, he is able to maintain pride and self-esteem when he must live within boundaries set up by external authority. The negative alternative is to acquire a sense of *shame and doubt*. To develop autonomy, the child must master two conflicting abilities: holding on and letting go. To master autonomy, a child should have an environment that can help him learn self-control and still acquire a sense of independence. The rules that are laid down for him and the restrictions that are placed upon him must be perceived by the child as meaningful, not simply to break his will or to inhibit his individuality. Without gaining a firm sense of autonomy, the child will lack discriminatory power and will have a tendency either to hold on to everything or to reject everything. The virtue that Erikson sees accompanying the acquisition of a sense of autonomy is *will*. The child gradually gains a knowledge of what he is able to do and what is expected of him. He learns to live with defeats and paradoxes. Though much of his life is out of his control, he persists in the exercise of free choice and restraint.

The third task of childhood is establishing a sense of *initiative*. The negative alternative is to acquire a sense of *guilt*. During this period, a child becomes more mobile, and his use of language increases dramatically. As a result, life takes on a host of possibilities for him, possibilities that he sees his parents enjoying. Along with his new mobility and use of language, the child's imagination operates at a new and exciting level. Preliminary sexual role identifications are made by the child. A boy or a girl at this stage hopes to become like father or mother respectively, or even *better* than they are. A child becomes much more active and especially intrusive. His inquisitiveness leads him in all directions. He takes on an aggressive attitude. In short, he begins to take initiative. On the other hand, a child may develop a stringent and vindictive conscience that constantly accuses him. In later life, such a person may be inhibited and self-restrictive, or he may seek to establish an unreal level of morality for others.

The virtue that the child learns if initiative wins out over guilt is *purpose*. If a sense of initiative is established, then the conscience has not become too restrictive. Guilt can be handled constructively. That is, he can see and accept where he has been wrong and can correct his behavior, and at the same time maintain a high level of self-esteem. Life makes sense and is challenging. Through his play, which is a rudimentary form of work, the child accepts the purposefulness of life and looks forward to participating in that purpose.

The final task of childhood is to attain a sense of *industry*. The negative alternative is a sense of *inferiority*. If a child is to become an adult, he will have to learn to be a worker and a provider. As the child grows older, he begins to put aside whimsical play and instead turns toward mastering the tools of his culture. In American society, this means he must go through an extensive educational process. If he is to develop a sense of industry instead of inferiority, the child must meet with some successes in this stage. If there is the mastery of this stage, there is established in the person a prototype of the successful and productive member of society. If the child does not gain a sense of accomplishment, he may develop a sense of inadequacy, inferiority, even despair. *Competence* is the name that Erikson gives to the virtue that results from gaining a sense of industry.[9] In our society, if not all societies, an individual's work has a lot to do with his feelings of worth. By being a productive member of society, an individual's self-estimate is enhanced. He gains a sense of worth through workmanship. This is sensed by the child.

Each person will be located at some point on a continuum between the positive and negative possibilities of each stage. Normally the positive will outweigh the negative; however, both will be operative to a degree in his life. The reader will have to decide for himself approximately where he is located on the continuum of each stage.

SUMMARY

Hereditary factors play a role in the development of the individual. It will be to the advantage of a youth if he both understands and accepts this fact. The physical growth that a person experiences at puberty, the development of the primary and secondary sex characteristics, and how he feels about these factors—both of which are beyond his control—also influence the shape of the young-ster. The environment of the individual, i.e., his family and his society, also contributes to his personality. Finally, how all of this is experienced by the developing child, as described by Erik Erikson, has profound implications for the personality of the youth as he encounters adolescence.

2

THE TASKS OF EARLY
AND MIDDLE ADOLESCENCE

The first chapter may have left the reader with the impression that much of life is determined, that it is beyond the conscious control of the individual. In many respects *we are our histories.* Yet in adolescence, a budding individual has the opportunity to make himself over according to his own specifications. From this vantage point, adolescence is a beautiful time of life. From another perspective, however, adolescence is a difficult time of life. Having broken loose from his moorings, an adolescent may feel uneasy, if not lost. The breaking-loose process can be perplexing and painful to a youth and to his parents alike. For the price, however, the adolescent gains his own chosen identity, his own will and purpose, and entry into adulthood.

Self-awareness and the Break from Parents

When a person is a child, his identification is with his parents. He sees himself as an extension of his parents. He thinks in terms of being a member of the family, the son or daughter of So-and-So. The guidelines for his life come from his parents. He does not question his own existence. Much of life is taken for granted.

When a person reaches adolescence he gains the power to step back, as it were, from his parents and his family, to see them more objectively and to see himself as an individual apart from them. He brings new critical power to bear on his relationship with his parents and on his own individuality. Instead of relying solely upon his parents for the many dimensions of his existence, he begins to look more at the world around him and particularly within himself. Slowly the adolescent changes his relationship with his parents, working toward less of an emotional tie to them. Sometimes a youth is conscious of his attempt to break away from parents, while at other times this is a subconscious activity. As the tie with his parents diminishes, the young person enters a stage where he reevaluates what he formerly believed and he begins to test new theories, new images, new systems, and new patterns of behavior. For these he turns to the external world, especially to his peers. With his peers he compares all that he previously took for granted. He begins to reshape his world, including his own identity.

Few adolescents disentangle themselves from their parents easily. Throughout childhood, parents were the authorities under whom the adolescent lived. They designed the world in which he lived. They outlined the values that he pursued. They shaped his identity. They molded his behavior patterns. The task he now faces in becoming aware of this widespread influence is formidable. He must develop a thorough understanding of his parents, family, and immediate environment and what effect these have had upon him. The more complete and rational this understanding, the better chance the adolescent has of becoming a self-directed person.

Gaining independence is a difficult but necessary task. To move away from one's parents and to take an objective look at them is the first step in going out on one's own. Though it is a small step, the adolescent realizes its implications and therefore approaches this step with some apprehension. Going one step farther and taking a critical stance toward one's parents takes an even greater amount of courage and often exacts a heavy cost in guilt and anxiety. Psychological withdrawal from parents—something that many young people find necessary in order to gain independence—often causes a type of mourning reaction in the adolescent, not easily recognized by him as such because his parents remain physically present. This causes moodiness and depression. There may be feelings of loneliness and isolation and moments of self-condemnation and despair.

The struggle for independence often entails a break with, if not a reaction or rebellion against, parents. If the youth is to find a place in the world, he first must handle his parents. He must adjust his view of them from the way in which he had viewed them in childhood and now must elevate himself to their size, *if not larger*. The young person often attempts to derogate his parents. He often is angry because he feels the world view that they assured him was correct is not shared by equally intelligent and acceptable people. Parental advice is no longer wanted; indeed, parents cannot say or do anything right. At the same time, however, many youth are not able to "go it alone" and need their parents. This ambivalence between needing and yet not wanting parents causes a confusion of emotions in the adolescent.

Normally in early adolescence the conscience weakens. This allows the young person to move away from childhood positions and patterns. With the thrust of puberty, the innate drives play a more dominant role. The result is that the adolescent has less executive control over himself, but now he has the possibility of gaining independence. This is a precarious time for the youth. Self-control threatens to break down. He is the victim of the rising and ebbing rhythms of instinctual drives on the one hand, and on the other hand the rising and ebbing rhythms of the ego's ability to exercise control. In late adolescence the person gains greater control and self-direction. For the moment, however, control and self-direction are elusive qualities.

The Infantile Conscience

The conscience that developed in the child, called the "infantile conscience," must give way to a conscience that serves the self-directed person in the complex world of adulthood. The infantile conscience is very restrictive and very rigid. It sees everything as black or white. For instance, playing in the street is bad, talking back to adults is bad, sexual experimentation or play is bad. The infantile conscience lacks the ability to modify, to handle shades of gray, or to change. That which once was bad remains bad. The infantile conscience views life from the perspective of a child. It will not adapt to the needs and life-style of the adolescent and the adult. If it remains active in the adolescent, it will block him from normal adulthood.

The infantile conscience enforces as "off limits" those things which were prohibited in childhood. Often parents make sure that prohibitions come through "loud and clear" to the child, but they do not make the same effort to help the child modify those views as he moves toward adolescence and adulthood. The result is that the infantile conscience punishes the person for what now is normal.

Part of adolescent rebellion is to throw off the last vestiges of the infantile conscience. Since his parents were the original determinants of his conscience, they become the symbol of the infantile conscience. Through his rebellion the adolescent hopes to rid himself of that part of his earlier life which is no longer needed or wanted. But getting rid of the infantile conscience is no easy task. Often an adolescent can be observed fluctuating between two poles: on the one hand, responding to his new energy, drives, and impulses; and on the other hand, being self-restrictive, self-punishing, and depressed. Peter Blos lists common polarities observed in the adolescent:

> Submission and rebellion, delicate sensitivity and emotional coarseness, gregariousness and withdrawal into solitude, altruism and egotism, boundless optimism and dejected hopelessness, intense attachments and sudden faithlessness, lofty ideals and petty argumentativeness, idealism and materialism, dedication and indifference, impulse acceptance and impulse rejection, voracious appetite, excessive indulgence and cruel self-negation (asceticism), physical exuberance and inert sluggishness.[10]

The adolescent cannot account for his moods and may feel that he is skirting chaos. In actuality he is attempting to find a balance between indulgence and control at an adult level as opposed to the restrictive life under the infantile conscience.

Increased Intellectual Ability

The physical growth and sexual maturation that a young person experiences usually capture his attention and the attention of those around him. Equally important for adulthood, but receiving less attention, is the intellectual growth that the young person experiences throughout adolescence. With this additional intellectual power, the young person gains the equipment necessary to handle the specific tasks of adolescence and the capacity and tools needed for adult life.

The adolescent's focus moves from himself to the larger external world. Instead of focusing on specific and concrete events or persons, the adolescent gains the ability to be more general and inclusive. For instance, he becomes interested in the political and social affairs of his community and his nation and takes an interest in the well-being of people whom he does not know personally. With his increased power, he is able to understand and work with concepts and systems of increasing complexity. For example, he will understand the power structure of his community or nation, or he will be able to raise searching ethical questions about the behavior of adults at some point or the course that his country is taking in some military activity.

One of the most important intellectual powers that the young person acquires is the ability to think abstractly. For instance, he can think about the vocation he will pursue. He can consider whether or not he has the ability for that occupation, what status that vocation has in the community, whether or not it is a meaningful occupation, and whether or not it will match his interests. All of this he can consider without actually taking the job. Or he may consider making a decision in which he may come into conflict with his parents. He may consider whether his position is morally right, how much guilt he will have if he goes ahead, what the consequences for his own sense of independence will be if he gives in to parental pressure. All of this can go through his mind without actualizing the decision. Stimulated by his broader interests and by his new drives, but without new controls working smoothly, the young person is somewhat vulnerable. Instead of having to live a hazardous existence through trial and error in actuality, now, with his ability to think abstractly, the young person can experiment *in his mind,* where the consequences are not so final.

With this new ability, the young person is able to construct for himself a value system. He is able to compare his ideas with those held by his parents, by other adults, and by his peers. Through an ordering of values and priorities, he is able to develop a comprehensive philosophy of life of his own. For example, an adolescent may disagree with the value his parents place on the acquisition of material goods, or he may take quite a different stand than do his parents on racial questions. Or, while his parents see the nation as their boundary line of concern, an adolescent may hold that national boundaries are artificial constructs which divide people in an arbitrary and potentially dangerous way. He no longer merely responds to his conscience, but educates it according to his own ideas. The adolescent develops a picture of the way he would like the world to be. He develops his own ethical system. For instance, whereas young men in earlier generations might kill the enemy in combat because of the political issues they believed were involved, an adolescent may believe that to kill even "the enemy" is a greater evil than to live under a given political system. Thus, he takes a different attitude toward war, or at least toward a particular war. Or, a youth may have attended a segregated grade school but may decide to attend an integrated high school because he feels that this is better for his society.

The adolescent comprehends time more fully than he did as a child. Instead of being limited to the recent past, the adolescent gains the ability to comprehend the vast historical past. He gains a feeling for the progression of time. With this he gains the ability to see life as meaningful. The adolescent is preoccupied, however, with the future, particularly with his own future. Both in his imagination and in reality—the latter mostly through his schoolwork—he looks for a place where he, in his independence and uniqueness, may play a role in history.

With his increased intellectual ability, the adolescent gains the faculty to probe and discuss an idea or a concept in depth. Frequently this amounts to an argument during which the young person will hold to an idea vigorously, partly as an exercise of his new equipment, partly to assert his independence, and partly because he may believe in it. The ability to *commit* himself to an idea or to a cause develops a little later.

The Search for an Identity

The phase-specific task of adolescence is the formation of an identity. The negative alternative is identity diffusion. An identity refers to the unique *and repetitive* way in which an individual's executive power (ego) synthesizes the various ingredients that make up the personality. This unique method of synthesis, or identity, must be formed and accepted by the individual and must be confirmed by the larger social sphere in which the person lives. There must be continuity between the self as the individual senses it and the self as others experience it. Identity is established when that identity makes sense to the individual and when, as that identity, the individual either finds or anticipates with confidence a unique place for himself in the social order.

Although establishing an identity implies the establishment of continuity and sameness in a person, nevertheless the identity of a person can and does change. The identity that a youth establishes in adolescence and early adulthood may change as he lives out his adult life. An identity is not fixed forever. It may be more accurate to talk about the adolescent's task of forming a "working identity" from which modifications will continue to spring. One factor causing such modifications is rapid social change. Indeed the more changes a society experiences, the more the identities of individuals living in that society are liable to change.

Adolescents vary in the degree of difficulty that they have with identity formation. With the sudden burst of puberty and its accompanying growth in size, change in shape, new sexual drives and characteristics, there is an obvious physical break with the past. With the desire to become autonomous and with the accompanying rejection of parental authority and views, there is also a psychological break with the past. Adolescents in this stage are in a no-man's-land, an uncomfortable feeling.

In this new stage, youth are preoccupied—sometimes morbidly, more often curiously—with what they appear to be in the eyes of others. They compare this with what they feel they are and with what, in the past, they had imagined they would be like. They also project what they feel like into the future and attempt to anticipate what it would be like to be this identity. In short, they try out—or on— identities.

It is in the formation of his identity that the adolescent is guided by his past and that he exercises his freedom to break from his past. Though the adolescent is shaped by his childhood and calls on past experiences and models, his new identity is not merely the sum of these. He also calls on his imagination and uses images that he sees in his larger world of peers and other adults. Teachers, coaches, parents of his friends, as well as his peers, offer him new possibilities. From past, present, and future (via imagination), the adolescent puts together a unique self which he finds both acceptable and workable. The adolescent also needs the recognition and approval of society. He must know that his gradual growth and transformation make sense and are acceptable to those around him.

The Moratorium

The adolescent is treated neither as a child nor as an adult. Adolescence is a time when a youth is supposed to take on the marks of an adult, but a time when he is forgiven relatively easily if he does not. For example, a young adult may drop out of school or quit his job and drift around the country without too much criticism, while this pattern in an older adult would be considered abnormal or pathological. Similarly, a youth could change jobs frequently without being questioned seriously, but the same behavior in an adult would cause people to raise questions about his stability. Society offers the adolescent what Erikson calls a "psychosocial moratorium." [11] This is a period when society allows the adolescent time to experiment, to make mistakes within reason, to put himself together and find his place in society. The law outlines less severe measures if the youth does go out-of-bounds. Society does, however, expect the young person to take on increasing responsibility, progress in the perfection of his skills, and move toward lasting commitments.

Even with this moratorium, the pressure of society bears down upon the adolescent. He is keenly aware that the task of forming his identity is formidable, that the length of time he is allotted is relatively short, that the decisions with which he is faced are far-reaching. The end of the moratorium, what Erikson calls the "psychosocial foreclosure," looms before him.

There are institutions within society that work for the youth in this period. Formal schooling serves as a supportive agency to the young. Here the rules and regulations keep in mind the stage of the youth. At the same time there are certain moments when he is reminded that his time will run out. For instance, the youth must decide in high school whether he will take the college preparation curriculum or some other. Increasingly, high schools give students the opportunity to major. Again, he must choose. Graduation from high school presents to those persons who will end their formal education at that level with the problem of choosing a vocation. Students who choose to go on to college must choose which college or university to attend, and in this choice there may be a decision about their future vocation. Once in college, the student is given a new lease on the moratorium, but not without important decisions about his future still facing him periodically. He must choose a major, a vocation, perhaps a marriage partner. The inability to decide on any one of these can present the young person with a crisis. Leaving the educational environment for the vocational world may loom before other young people as a fearful experience. It is the seeming finality of such decisions which most bothers the young.

Military service is another institution that serves the young during this period, at least during peacetime. Often the period to be served is two years; sometimes it is more. It gives him an unhurried period of time to ponder key decisions, including decisions about vocation and marriage.

Young men often feel the pressure over their vocational futures. Young ladies tend to feel the pressure over both vocation and marriage. Society has conflicting and confusing expectations of a young lady. In school she is to plan for a vocation. Yet society assumes that she will get married and it puts pressure on her to marry. If no marriage plans develop for a girl, she must put more emphasis on her vocation. She may be happy over this turn of events or she may not. If marriage plans do develop, then frequently vocational plans go unfulfilled or are happily placed second, depending upon how she feels about each of these possibilities. The future can be just as confusing and fearful to a young lady as it is to a young man.

Young people who experience apprehension or fear over their future give evidence of a variety of symptoms. Depression is common, as is anxiety. Frequently there is a slowing down of the physical and psychological processes. Some young people can become quite immobile.

A young man in his junior year in college succumbed to this type of pressure. He became extremely depressed. He could no longer attend his classes. He was immobilized by fear. He espoused a hippie philosophy quite unconvincingly and unnaturally. Because he had a "good boy" self-image up to that point, he felt very guilty about his condition. He could not decide for certain about a major. He simply could not move ahead with any of the majors that he had entertained. This posed a problem, since he had to choose a major by his junior year. In addition, his fiancée had recently broken their engagement. He took this as a blow to his masculinity. With his masculinity and vocation in doubt and with society putting pressure on him, both because of his age and educational status, this young man could not move ahead. The future was rolling in on him too rapidly.

For most persons, the moratorium provides them with sufficient time to form an identity and accomplish the other work that is necessary to attain adulthood. As the individual establishes an identity, he experiences a sense of well-being. He feels more at home in his body, he knows more clearly where he is going, he feels confident that he can handle the future, and he senses the recognition of his accomplishments and ambitions by the society around him.

Identity Diffusion

The negative alternative of identity formation is identity diffusion (confusion). Identity diffusion is the result of an inability to put together from the various sources—past, present, and future—an acceptable and workable identity. Because of an inability to define himself, to relate sexually with others, to decide on an occupation, to engage in competition with his peers or with adults—any one or a combination of these—a youth may not be able to move ahead with his psychosocial work. Indeed, he may experience the collapse of the psychological work that he had accomplished. The future may loom as an impossible object to handle. The decisions he faces weigh heavily upon him. When he avoids making these decisions, however, he experiences feelings of isolation and shame.

Erikson has identified patterns of diffusion and reactions to diffusion: time diffusion, diffusion of industry, negative identity, and identity resistance.[12]

If there is a long-delayed or prolonged adolescence, a person may experience a disturbance in his experience of time. He may have both a sense of urgency about time and a disregard of time. There is a slowing down of the entire life-style in such a person. Every moment is not only hard to face but hard to let go.

A co-ed with whom I counseled periodically over the four years she was in college experienced time diffusion; indeed, she had many of the symptoms usually associated with schizophrenia. There was a blank look on her face and a slowness about her pace. She was indifferent to time, frequently coming in long after the appointed hour. She had difficulty with even the smallest decision and openly stated that she wished she could stop the world for a while. She often came in, slouched in a chair, stated that she didn't know why she came in, and waited for me to pick up the conversation from there. Her senior piano recital had to be postponed twice because she was not ready.

Choosing an occupation was particularly troublesome to her. She pondered being a music major. She had enjoyed music as a child, and her mother was interested in music. She toyed with mathematics as a major. Her father was good at math and enjoyed it. She thought about going into social work where she could work with retarded children. She had a brother who was retarded. Though she took all the required courses to go into teaching, she failed to develop a portfolio of credentials necessary for job application.

In her senior year she dated a young man steadily. He asked her to marry him. This posed an additional problem. She was afraid of intimacy and the finality of a decision about marriage. She told the young man not to date her any longer, but when he persisted, she continued the courtship. The possibility of marriage was confusing to her. On the one hand, she could avoid the vocational choice with which she was having so much difficulty. On the other hand, she was afraid of the finality of marriage; she felt she could not make that type of commitment. At one point in our conversations when we were handling some of these topics, she suddenly became angry. She sensed that she was moving ahead and she resented, and possibly feared it.

In a mild form, time diffusion merely brings a mistrust and fear of time. In more serious cases, time—those people and institutions associated with it—may be gravely mistrusted and feared. In severe cases, there may be an attempt to slow down time through catatonic immobility or even through death.

Sometimes identity diffusion is experienced in the form of diffusion of industry, an upset in the person's sense of industry. There may be an inability to concentrate on required or suggested tasks or there may be a detrimental preoccupation with one activity to the exclusion of other, more important tasks. For example, instead of studying, a young man may spend his time working on his car, building an electronics kit, playing cards, or working on the school newspaper. Often a fear of competition sends a person off on some obscure project where he is not in competition with either adults or peers. For example, while all the other members of an American history class will write a paper on the major battles of the Civil War, one student will write a paper on the history of firearms up to the Civil War. Or, while all the other members of a history class may write a paper on the contribution of the Mayan civilization to contemporary Mexican culture, one student will build to scale a model of a Mayan city, carefully detailing the unique architectural features of the Mayan culture. Frequently the feeling of inadequacy that such a person has is quite inappropriate. Such people often have great ability. They are the victims of their own idealism and are unwilling to settle for anything less than perfection. Such a person may feel that society does not have a niche for him. His experimentation with play in childhood and with work earlier in adolescence may have been frustrated. He may feel inadequate for life.

An immature-looking boy was referred to the counseling center because of bizarre sexual thoughts, which he had expressed in the dormitory, as he later explained, in order to be accepted by his peers. Among the faculty, this boy was known for the thoroughness with which he did research projects, albeit research projects on remote and quite unimportant subjects. He avoided competition with his fellow students by choosing remote topics on which he would not be compared with his peers. At the time of my last conversation, this boy was planning to become a curator of a museum.

Another dimension of identity diffusion is negative identity. If the demands and the ideals of the parents or of the community seem beyond the reach of the adolescent, and if there is an inability to form an identity on the basis of what the young person sensed was being prescribed for him, he may reject those ideals and roles in favor of a negative identity. Indeed, he may treat with acid disdain any aspect or all parts of the role or roles that were suggested to or urged on him. He may reject masculinity or femininity, as the case may be, as well as the nationality, class membership, values, religion, etc., of his parents. Often there is a dislike for and rejection of everything familiar and an idealizing of everything that is unfamiliar.

In such a case, a young person is able to get a clearer picture of, or feels that he is able to accomplish, those things which were *prohibited* instead of those things which were prescribed. What he was *not supposed to be* he now finds he can become. Instead of attaining a positive identity, he acquires a negative identity. Erikson points out:

> Many a late adolescent, if faced with continuing diffusion, would rather be nobody or somebody bad, or indeed, dead—and this totally, and by free choice —than be not-quite-somebody.[13]

Through taking on a negative identity, the adolescent attempts to gain mastery over diffusion. He also succeeds in asserting his autonomy. He avoids regression and shame.

A co-ed from a small, homogeneous community provides us with an example of a negative identity. As a young girl she was known community-wide for her excellent academic ability and musical talent. She entered college on a scholarship for each. When she came to college it was assumed that she would major in music, and she did, for the first year. She did very well throughout most of her freshman year both academically and in the musical productions in which she participated. Toward the end of her freshman year, however, she lost interest in music, and her academic work deteriorated. At the begin-

ning of her sophomore year she changed her major to
chemistry, with the intent of going into some phase of
medicine. At first she did well. As the year wore on, however, she cut classes, missed tests, and did not turn in her
work. During the summer between her sophomore and
her junior year, she did social work in a special black
ghetto project in a large city. She became enthusiastic
about the work and at the same time became bitter about
her family and community background. She became very
vocal about her community's racial prejudice. She identified closely with a number of black participants in the
project.

When she returned to college in the fall she was sullen.
Eventually she dropped out of college. She went to live
on the fringe of a large university, where she associated
with a racially mixed group of people whose life-style was
completely different from and repugnant to the ideals of
her parents and community. This is a case where the musi-
cian and student image that the girl had gained in childhood was unacceptable to her in adolescence; nor could
she center her identity around other positive and acceptable substitutes. The alternative to continued diffusion and
despair was a negative identity.

Faced with forces that threaten to swallow him completely, an adolescent may engage in what Erikson calls
identity resistance. In order to protect the little ego
strength that he has acquired, and fearing that even this
little bit may be swallowed up by the stronger figures and
forces around him, the adolescent regresses to rock bottom
in an attempt to guard his autonomy. He retreats to a safe
hiding place from which he can observe life and look for
a safe place where he might attempt a comeback. In his
regression he searches once again for the trustworthiness

of life because in his initial search for an identity he came to mistrust life completely. Such a person wishes to retrace his steps in order to make a second, and more successful, attempt at identity formation.

Desirous as the adolescent may be to form his identity, he may choose diffusion over making what appears to him an irreversible decision about his identity. Commitment involves repudiation, as does identity formation, and the adolescent finds repudiation difficult. Repudiation is the rejection of ideas, values, behavior patterns, and identifications that are contradictory or extraneous to the tentative core values or budding identity of an individual.

The commitment involved in identity formation takes on the appearance of surrender and accountability to others. Especially in a culture of rapid social change, youth wish to remain open to the new, the unlikely, even the forbidden. There is resistance to repudiation and a tendency to play it "cool," to push back commitment and to forestall foreclosure. This also forestalls identity formation. Repudiation is essential to identity formation.

The Move Toward Heterosexuality

One of the significant moves that the adolescent has to make is the one from bisexuality to heterosexuality. Boys and girls move toward heterosexuality by way of a more general move from the internal world toward the external world, away from passivity and toward activity. Some of this movement is already accomplished in preadolescent years. Boys move more slowly and cautiously toward heterosexuality than do girls. Early in adolescence the youth exchanges his identification with familiar love objects that are related to his internal world for love objects from the larger sphere of the external world.

At first a young adolescent turns toward a friend or a group of friends. As an adolescent moves away from his parents, friends take on new importance. They usually take an idealized form. They are seen to have features that the adolescent himself would like to have, and through the friendship, the adolescent has these features by proxy. In this way, friends make up for the missing perfections of the self. The friendship supports the weak and precarious, but budding, self.

With support from the external world, the adolescent focuses a great deal of attention on himself. He may be both arrogant and rebellious toward his parents. Parents experience the fate of a fallen idol. Actually the adolescent is attempting to build up his own self-esteem and establish his own worth and independence. What the external world thinks of the adolescent is of vital importance to him.

At this stage the adolescent's feelings run deeply. An adolescent feels as though no one else in history has ever felt as deeply as he presently does about someone or something. A girl's diary often records the feelings that she experiences and wishes to keep forever. In her diary a girl records a life that is largely in her mind; it is filled with fantasy and experimentation. Heterosexual activity is played out harmlessly through her daydreams. This rich fantasy life performs a valuable service by providing experimentation without the finality of reality.

In addition to fantasy but much more risky than fantasy, however, is the experimentation that adolescents carry out in reality. They exert themselves in physical and emotional exercises, in experiments in endurance and daring. For instance, a young man may take a construction job and work to his very limits to see how he compares with others and to find out his work limits. A girl may let her emotions run to extreme in a love affair just to see what emotional capacity she has. Or a group of young people in two automobiles may engage in daring acts, such as racing or driving dangerously close to one another, or in the direction of one another, or to find out who is the most daring. They try out systems of thought, patterns of behavior, attitudes and practices that skirt, and sometimes break through, their tentative emotional boundaries. Lacking critical judgment and physical and emotional control, but propelled by their new energies, many adolescents actually live a precarious life. In this stage, adolescents are searching for the boundaries of their abilities and plumbing the depths of their emotions. Before they can develop an identity, they must find out what they have to work with.

By the time the person has reached middle adolescence, the final transition to a heterosexual orientation is made. Relationships with and attachments to persons of the opposite sex become normative. Before the final move is made to this firm heterosexual orientation, the adolescent's emotional life is shaky. Especially among boys, there is a fear of homosexuality during this period. This fear can be disconcerting and it may linger and undermine the boy's self-confidence. For both boys and girls the move is not always made easily. The break with the past has a finality about it that may bring apprehension, anxiety, and sometimes depression. The past is known and therefore safe, the future is unknown and therefore unsafe. Without knowing the outcome of his identity, the adolescent cannot be sure that he will be attractive to someone of the opposite sex. Usually, however, the adolescent sees a new, exciting, and hopeful future on the horizon. The adolescent reaches that "point of no return" and moves firmly into heterosexuality.

SUMMARY

In early adolescence, the young person severs his earlier emotional ties with his parents and gains a more objective view of them and of himself. He may experience some apprehension as he makes his first move into uncharted territory. Yet he proceeds because he seeks independence and a unique identity. Any vestiges of the infantile conscience must be removed. He must develop a more adaptive and flexible conscience. He experiences intellectual growth which helps him with his struggle for independence. The major task of adolescence is the formation of a unique identity. To gain this identity the adolescent calls not only on his past identifications but increasingly on the larger world of his peers and other adults. From this combination of models he shapes one that he can accept and that society finds acceptable. Recognizing that he faces a difficult task, society offers the adolescent a moratorium, a time when he can experiment without fear of the finality of his decisions and actions. Some adolescents experience varying forms of identity diffusion when they cannot seem, through a process of repudiation and positive choice, to form an identity. During early and middle adolescence, youth also move from a bisexual orientation to a heterosexual orientation, and thus move one step closer to adulthood.

3

THE MOODS, FEELINGS, AND DEFENSES
OF MIDDLE ADOLESCENCE

Adolescents are often an enigma to their parents and some-times to themselves as well. Since adolescence follows the rather quiet stage of late childhood, the relationship that now exists between parent and adolescent may be in stark contrast with the relationship that prevailed before. With all that is new and still developing within him, and all that remains unknown to him about himself and his future, the adolescent doesn't quite know what to think of himself. He cannot give a rational explanation to himself, much less to anyone else, as to why he says the things he says and does the things he does. The purpose of this chapter is to describe some of the moods and feelings the adoles-cent has and to describe as well some of the defenses on which the adolescent relies during this stage.

Anxiety

Because of the particular stage of development that he has reached at adolescence, with the new physical urges, the emotional changes that he experiences, and the psy-chological work that he must perform, the adolescent is a frequent victim of fear and anxiety.

Though fear and anxiety are similar, there is an important difference between them. Fear is apprehension over a specified danger. For example, a person may fear that he is going to get a low grade in math, or he may fear that he will not finish an assignment on time. Anxiety is diffuse apprehension; it cannot be related to any particular object. As a result, it is more difficult for the adolescent to handle. In anxiety, the person experiences a threat to a value that he holds to be essential to his physical, psychological, or social well-being. He may doubt that he will be accepted by his peers, or he may experience apprehension that he will not be able to establish his identity firmly enough to be independent from a dominant parent. Because anxiety is objectless and yet is experienced as a threat to the core of one's being, it may cause the adolescent to feel trapped, even overwhelmed.[14]

While temporarily serving as an academic dean, I witnessed an acute attack of anxiety in a co-ed. Earlier in the day she had been accused of plagiarism by one of her professors. I had known this girl for some time. She lived by a "good girl" image. Though she was not a top student, she was well behaved, quiet, and religious. When she came in to see me, she could hardly talk. She wondered what the college would do to her. In the same breath she informed me that she had already called her parents to have them come to get her. I indicated that the charge against her did not warrant her dropping out of school and that the college, in the case of a first offense, would probably do little more than warn her and inform her what plagiarism is and how it can be avoided. She could not be persuaded to stay in college. She indicated that she could not live here with this on her record. I told her that such cases of plagiarism were common and that people so charged could maintain their dignity and self-respect. Nothing could change her mind. I asked her to have her parents come to see me when they arrived. She indicated that this would do no good. She felt she could not stay another day. This minor offense became a threat to her total being.

Insight about the nature of anxiety is offered by a number of theorists. For Paul Tillich, anxiety is the threat of non-being.[15] In a physical sense, this is death; in a psychological sense, this is the threat of meaninglessness. The threat that life was meaningless came to a freshman girl who sought out the counseling center about six weeks after her arrival in the fall. She told me that she came from a good family. She recited how close her family was and all the things the members did together. She emphasized the wonderful things her father did. In despair, however, she told me that, just before she left for college, her father informed her "out of the blue" that he was going to divorce her mother and marry another woman.

This co-ed was faced with many new ideas at college, on the one hand; and, on the other hand, all the ideas and principles that she had been taught by her father were now in question because he himself was denying them. She was at a loss to know what was right and what was wrong. What was she to believe in? On what principles should she base her life? The confusion of ideas that she faced because of her father's action and as a result of encountering opinions differing from her own at college made this girl ask whether there was any meaning to life. Not knowing which ideas she should use to guide her life, she found herself filled with anxiety.

Kurt Goldstein's concept of anxiety is similar. Anxiety is caused by the threat of the dissolution of the individual's personality. Fear usually precedes anxiety. When a certain level of fear is reached, fear changes to anxiety, to an apprehension that threatens to engulf the whole person.[16] Mowrer holds that anxiety results when, as a result of the lack of appropriate action, the individual fears the removal of love and approval by important persons in his life. When these fears become repressed, they change into anxiety.[17] Otto Rank holds that anxiety results from man's pursuit of autonomy. Each act of autonomy entails an act of individuation, i.e., separation from others. Man fears losing his individuality, on the one hand, and, on the other hand, he fears being separated from others.[18] How secure or how threatened a person was in his early life has a great deal to do with how safe or how secure he feels in later years, and therefore with how much anxiety he experiences in later years.

From these insights into the nature and the origin of anxiety, it is not difficult to understand why adolescents experience a great deal of anxiety. With their newly developed cognitive powers, young people find themselves questioning many of the ideas and positions that they received from their parents and begin looking for new ideas and positions. They experience both guilt over questioning their parents' views and anxiety as they seek to replace those views with ones they can call their own. In my years of teaching in the department of religion, I observed many young people go through the agonizing process of confronting "foreign" ideas, placing these alongside positions which they had inherited, and deciding which they would hold. For instance, some students found it threatening to hear a professor of religion take a position contrary to that of the literal six-day creation, or hold the position that Moses may not have authored the Pentateuch, or compare the classical prophets with current prophetic personalities, such as Martin Luther King, Jr., in contemporary American society.

The adolescent understands full well the far-reaching implications of this process. He is not sure of his capacity to handle such grave matters on his own. He is putting in jeopardy his relationship with those who taught him. He is questioning the image of God he has had and the estimate of reality on which he has lived. This amounts to severing his ties with the past while his future is still in doubt.[19]

Developing a unique and workable identity is at the heart of adolescent anxiety. The adolescent must shape himself. If his identity was more or less provided for him in childhood, this is no longer the case. Now he has the ability and the responsibility to gain a perspective on what he has been, who his parents are, and whether or not he accepts them and what they stand for. Without a fully formed self-concept, he must become autonomous. Without much of a base on which to operate, he must make important decisions. These decisions concern who he is and who he will become. The adolescent has "himself" in his hands. He bears the responsibility to create a significant, respectable, and free self. Being critical of his parents brings more responsibility on him to make something of himself. The values he chooses, his behavior, his vocational plans, his dating partners, are all a part of his solution to his quest for identity. And entertaining the thought of sidestepping these decisions only gives him shame. When he does decide on a self-image, there are always lingering doubts as to the adequacy and correctness of this image.

His physical growth and sexual development are other causes of anxiety. A rapid rate of growth may cause the young person to lose touch with himself, not knowing who he is or what he looks like to others, or what he will finally look like. The lack of growth and the possibility of small stature can be a source of anxiety to some, while largeness and/or obesity may be a problem for others. The newly felt sexual urges can be very traumatic. Here the young person must make a complete about-face, going from a childhood suppression of such urges to an adolescent acceptance of them. This is not always done easily. As the person grows older, society expects that he will have more intimate contact with the opposite sex, and yet he may not be ready for such a level of intimacy. Whether or not a person is attractive to the opposite sex and whether or not he will be considered very masculine or feminine are areas of doubt and anxiety in youth.

Threatened as often as he is by anxiety, the adolescent may attempt to defend himself. Defenses against anxiety take many forms. Some young people attempt to avoid anxiety by avoiding the danger situation. Through conformity they may avoid uniqueness and individuality and thus attempt to avoid anxiety. As a consequence, such young people limit their thoughts and actions and draw in the boundaries of their lives to safer dimensions. Other young people may shift the focus from themselves to others. They may be authoritarian and thus attempt to control others. They may engage in sadistic or destructive acts toward others, hoping in that way to avoid anxiety.

A junior co-ed came in for counseling complaining of "the shakes." She cried frequently, was filled with fear, couldn't concentrate, and was extremely agitated. She had been dating a particular young man during her years at college; indeed, she had known him before she came to college. She came from a middle-class family. She was an excellent student, generally attractive and pleasant, an only child, and, by her own admission, was spoiled and self-centered. In counseling, she expressed a large number of concerns; however, she focused mostly on the question of whether or not she would be able to maintain her own autonomy and independence in her marriage to this young man.

The family into which she planned to marry was an upper-class family. The father was reported to be the dominant figure. The young man she planned to marry had all the marks of wealth and therefore she had no fears concerning whether or not she would be provided with the comforts of life. Her complaints centered on the fact that she felt her boyfriend was under the domination of his father. She complained that he was too passive and not independent or aggressive enough. This lack of aggressiveness was evident, she claimed, in their sexual life.

A number of things suggested to me that the picture was perhaps not as simple as she painted it. My observation of the young man did not corroborate the passivity and lack of independence about which she had spoken. Secondly, the young lady was at the center of an episode in her dormitory. Another girl, whom she disliked, was exercising more leadership in the dormitory than was she. The girls no longer jumped at her every command. She felt that her place in the dormitory, particularly among her friends, was slipping. Finally, I was aware that her boyfriend was graduating at mid-year and was planning to return to his home area to work, leaving her behind with one and one-half years of college to complete. As it turned out, she left college at the same time that he completed his work.

In restrospect, it appeared to me that because of the diffuse apprehensiveness of anxiety, she could not isolate and handle her problem constructively. She projected onto her boyfriend her own anxieties. She lashed out at others because of her own fears over autonomy and independence.

Anxiety may show up in a variety of ways and to a variety of degrees. Emotionally, it may cause interference with the thought processes through the loss of concentration or a break in a train of thought, in preoccupation, or in a blocking of communication. In more severe cases there may be paralysis of thought and action. Physically, there may be a change in the tone of voice and in the tempo of speech, a change in posture or motion. In cases of severe anxiety there may be increased perspiration, tremor, a sensation of vomiting, change in heartbeat and pulse rate as well as in respiration. With severe anxiety, the person may panic and/or develop a psychosis. When there appears to be no escape from the anxiety, there may be temporary disintegration of the personality.

Guilt and Shame

Again, because of the stage of life he is in, with its unique psychological work, particularly the task of breaking away from parents, the adolescent experiences a great deal of guilt. Often anxiety and guilt are confused. Thomas C. Oden differentiates between guilt and anxiety:

> Guilt always refers through memory to something which is already past, just as anxiety always refers oppositely to some possibility which has not yet occurred. They work in opposite ways, one through memory, the other through imagination.[20]

In the case of guilt, the person experiences feelings of tension and pain when he has denied or has broken a value which he and/or significant others in his life hold.

Guilt and anxiety work hand in hand through the conscience to form the individual's control system. An adolescent's conscience is the product of his early experiences with important persons, usually his parents. Values and behavior patterns received from these figures are internalized. These are meant to guide the person throughout his life, giving him both "oughts" and "ought nots." When an adolescent commits an "ought not," he experiences the pain of guilt. When he thinks about committing an "ought not," he experiences the pain of anxiety. The conscience has a "before the fact" warning system whereby the conscience arouses anxiety in anticipation of the loss of approval of self and/or others, and there is an "after the fact" punitive system by which the person experiences the loss of approval for having committed a forbidden act.

Shame is also closely associated with guilt. Though shame is defined differently by different theorists, Gerhart Picr's definition appears to me to be the most helpful. For Pier, *guilt* is the result of the transgression of something prohibited, while *shame* is the result of failure to reach goals or ideals.[21] Shame has to do with self-doubt and a lack of trust in oneself. Shame leads to feelings of inferiority and isolation and goes even deeper into the individual than guilt. It is more serious to be an outcast in one's own eyes than to be condemned by society.[22]

Both shame and guilt are experienced frequently by adolescents. To become independent from their parents, adolescents have to conquer their infantile conscience as well as go against their training at any number of points. To establish their unique identity, they must go through the lonely and frightening process of shedding past identifications and establish a new identification for which they alone are responsible. They must develop their own morality and feel confident in it. They must break childhood patterns and experiment, in actuality or in their imagination, with new patterns.

Because young people set up idealistic standards, they easily acquire guilt and shame for breaking these standards. Young people tend to be unrealistic or uninformed about the force of their new emotions. They find that the power of their emotions, as they experiment with them, is sometimes greater than their control over those emotions. For example, a young man may claim that young people are better drivers than older people and may dispute the high automobile insurance rates that young people must pay. That same young man will experience shame when he wrecks his automobile because he misjudged a curve that he was trying to negotiate at high speed. Most young people during this period of identity formation feel that they must prove themselves. Often their failures stand out in stark relief in their own minds. Prone to daydreams, youth realize that they cannot live up to their hopes and dreams. Because young people convict others on the basis of their idealistic standards, they are unable to forgive themselves.[23]

The adolescent is faced with the task of finding a unique place for himself in society. He often does not feel acceptable as he is. He is as yet incompletely formed. He is in a state of becoming. He must form himself into someone acceptable. Until he does, he questions his worth and experiences shame. He may wish that he were someone different or, at worst, that he did not exist. If he gains acceptance, usually in the form of gaining friends, his shame diminishes. If he is unsuccessful in developing friends, his shame increases. Instead of turning to friends, he may turn to academic achievement or to work. What the adolescent senses that others think about him or feel toward him has a great deal to do with how he thinks or feels about himself. Generally speaking, an adolescent will search for a situation in which he can meet with acceptance and success and therefore feel good about himself. Each attempt that ends in failure increases his measure of shame.

As young people establish their value system and develop their identity, they may experience shame of a different sort. Young people may experience shame over the values held by their parents. They may also experience shame over the values and the conduct of the society into which they were born.[24] There seems to be a deep current of shame running through the youth of our country, especially among college students, over the values and policies of our country.

A young man, the son of immigrant parents, suffered from guilt and shame. Though very able, the father held a "menial" job in this country. The mother had little education and attempted to maintain her Old World customs and enforce them in the family. The young man carried a great deal of shame over his parents. At the same time, he fell short of his own ideals. He compared himself with an older brother both in his studies and in sports and came out on the short end. Nor was he accepted by his peers. He was sullen much of the time and caustic in the few comments he uttered. In addition to suffering from shame over his parents and over his own lack of success, he felt guilty over his behavior, which was in sharp contrast to what his parents sought from him. In short, this young man gave his parents a great deal of pain and he experienced much pain within himself. What he found most painful to discuss was his lack of acceptance by his own peers.

Young people walk a tightrope between guilt and shame. In breaking away from parents they are vulnerable to feelings of guilt. If they do not develop this autonomy, young people are vulnerable to feelings of shame. Few young people are able to avoid experiencing these feelings.

Other Moods and Feelings

Some adolescents become involved in a traumatic and seemingly life-and-death struggle between dependence and independence. Panic proportions in this struggle are not hard for an adolescent to reach. Adolescents tend to draw the lines of battle very sharply, making their independence from parents, usually one parent, an all-or-nothing situation. In the mind of the adolescent, the parent takes on monsterlike proportions. In the adolescent's mind, if he does not get out from under the domination of the parent, he will never amount to anything. His is a desperate attempt to escape shame. In this condition the adolescent lacks the capacity to modify his stance, to be satisfied with gradual progress toward independence. A parent may be baffled over the anger directed toward him by his son or daughter. In some cases it is not so much how dominating the parent *actually is,* but how much under the domination of the parent *the adolescent feels he is.* Sometimes an adolescent will hide any anger he has toward a parent and direct that anger toward himself. His is a struggle for self-respect.

A young man who had a nervous breakdown the previous year while at another college came in for counseling about two weeks after the fall term began. He admitted that he had been advised not to reenroll in college, at least temporarily. He was both anxious and depressed. In talking with him, I discovered that he had drawn the lines of his success or failure *as a person* on the basis of whether or not he would be able to remain away from home and obtain a college education. And this was the last try he would give himself. He had mixed feelings about his parents. On the one hand, he knew he needed them; on the other hand, he resented them. More than this, however, he hated himself for not being able to get along without them. He saw the situation as either/or: either he was going to establish his independence once for all in the coming weeks, or he would be a complete failure. His continuing need for his parents had become an obsession.

Another young man felt very strongly about his mother's overweening attitude and behavior toward him. He reached a state of immobility. Not able to attend his classes, he was sent home for psychiatric care. While at home he wrecked the new car, which his parents had recently given him, in an act of repudiation of his parents and perhaps as a symbolic act of self-disgust as well. When he re-enrolled several terms later, his mother indicated that she had interrupted his psychiatric visits because of the bizarre theories that the psychiatrist had about her son's problems. Obviously the psychiatric care her son was receiving threatened the mother. Shortly after enrolling, the young man stated that he had made a girl pregnant and planned to marry her. Again this was a symbolic act of repudiation of his mother and an attempt to establish in her mind, and perhaps in his own, his independence and his masculinity as well.

Another problem that plagues some adolescents and

becomes a problem for parents, teachers, and community alike is underachievement. Underachievement is a symptom of emotional conflicts that lie beneath the surface. It may be caused simply by preoccupation with other matters that are confusing to the adolescent and that, because these matters are important in his struggle for autonomy and identity, take precedence over schoolwork. Underachievement may appear when a person feels lonely and feels the lack of concern by others. It may also develop when achievement seems meaningless to the adolescent. Underachievement may result from a need to fail, even if there is an accompanying need to achieve. It may be the result of rebellion against authority in an achievement-oriented society. It may result from feelings of inferiority. A person may not try, lest in trying his best, he finds that his best is not good enough. Therefore he avoids a final label of "failure" by not trying. Underachievement may result from a repression of aggressive drives that the adolescent is unable to handle. Whatever its cause, underachievement is a factor in the lives of a large number of adolescents.

Defenses

Having looked at the tasks that face the adolescent, along with the moods and feelings he frequently has, we now look at some of the defenses the adolescent uses to aid him in this stage.

Probably the most common type of defense that a young person uses to handle his new energy is sublimation, i.e., directing his energies into substitute activities. By engaging in these substitute activities, the youth not only defends himself against his burgeoning energies but he also experiments with his identity, gains experience with his equipment and abilities, receives personal gratification, gains approval from adult society and acceptance by his peers. These substitute activities protect him from uncomfortable feelings and frightening acts and at the same time allow him to release his energy. Any form of sports is perhaps the most common substitute for both boys and girls. Tinkering with cars, holding a part-time job, sewing, cheerleading, participating in musical groups and church youth group activities are other common substitutes.

The peer group is a strategic form of defense for young people. For one thing, the individual adolescent is able to defend himself from guilt feelings by projecting those feelings onto the group with which he identifies. This is called the socialization of guilt.[25] As a result, the adolescent does not have to bear that guilt alone. There is safety from overwhelming guilt in the gang.

Secondly, there is safety from criticism from the adult world in the peer group. Adolescents, especially recently, have formed a sort of mutual aid society by developing their own culture. Through uniformism, i.e., through following rigidly a common dress code and by using "in" language, youth set up the boundaries of their culture.[26] The peer group tolerates the moods, thoughts, feelings, and actions common to adolescents. Because each adolescent is experiencing his share of these, he does not criticize his mates. The group tolerates the silence and sullenness that the adult world finds so difficult to handle. The peer group through sheer numbers provides safety from the adult world.

While protecting the adolescent from the adult world, the peer group provides him with other benefits. It protects the adolescent from inner loneliness and feelings of strangeness. The group provides the adolescent with a sounding board for any far-out thoughts he may have. It provides him with answers to questions that perplex the adolescent. The group establishes a code of ethics and behavior and gives the youth a peer, rather than an adult, standard. This helps the young person to shape a new conscience. In the group the youth finds solace through the similar sufferings of others.

The telephone is a particularly useful instrument for the adolescent peer group. Because it provides the adolescent with easy access to his peers, it has been referred to as the "dial-a-peer" phenomenon.[27] The telephone helps the adolescent to handle the boredom, loneliness, and anxiety that he experiences at home through easy contact with his peers. It also helps the adolescent to keep firm the boundary lines between the peer and the adult world. He is able to maintain solidarity with his mates even while being physically distant from them.

Handling their new sexual drives and interests is difficult for some adolescents, especially in the earlier years. Boys may become quite hostile toward girls. This may take the form of belittling girls, avoiding them, teasing them, or it may go as far as aggressive acts toward them. Girls may turn to tomboyish behavior as a form of defense. As a part of this tomboyishness, a girl may engage in various forms of athletics. Girls often develop clannish friendships with other girls, spend a great deal of time grooming themselves, and engage in a rich fantasy life.

Two of the most common forms of defense against sexuality, especially among girls, are asceticism and intellectual pursuits. The ascetic and intellectual approaches to life are idealized in the mind of the adolescent and made into lofty virtues in order to avoid sexual impulses and heterosexual activity. The intellectual defense is particularly easy to adopt because of the importance of education in American society. The adolescent will receive the praise of adult society even if he is not readily accepted in his peer world. And the intellectual defense is not without other values. During this stage, the young person may develop lasting interests, discover particular talents, move in the direction of a particular vocation because of his intellectual focus. Asceticism, on the other hand, is a more repressive form of defense that contributes much less to the development of the adolescent.

It has been my experience that as the person moves toward the middle and late adolescent stages, however, he sees that his intellectual defense has isolated him from his peers and that he has been left "without any of the goodies," as one counselee put it. The person sees that other youth are able to handle their drives. He also is moving toward the age when adult society, which he had been responding to, expects him to find a marriage partner, yet he is not even dating. Many young people find themselves wanting to change their life-style at that point, but they do not always know how. They have had little experience relating to the opposite sex, at least in any broadly "sexual" sense. Indeed, they had convinced themselves that their intellectual pursuits were of far greater value. Their conscience does not let them reverse values and life-styles easily.

A freshman girl with whom I counseled had a very negative attitude toward her body even though, or perhaps because, she was both pretty and shapely. Before coming to college she had not had any dates, in spite of the fact that her parents had encouraged her. When she came to college she began to allow her imagination to entertain sexual thoughts. These thoughts gave her no end of guilt feelings. Her infantile conscience reinforced her asceticism. After the Thanksgiving recess, she told me that she had talked to her mother about sex during the vacation. She discovered that her mother was much more open about sex, including the subject of premarital sex, than was she. She found this fact very difficult to handle.

Another girl with whom I counseled had formed, but was trying to discard, an intellectual defense against sexuality. I had known this girl for several years and had been able to observe the image she had portrayed for several years on the campus. She was the champion of many causes, a leader of intellectual discussions, and identified by her peers as a "brain," even though she did not earn very high grades. She gave out anything but warm sexual signals.

She began the conversation by saying that she had questions about her sexuality. Though a senior, she was just beginning to recognize, rather than repress, her sexual feelings. She saw that other girls could handle their sexual feelings. Because she had confusing thoughts and feelings about sex and because she had not had any dates, she secretly feared she might be homosexual.

We talked at great length about her thoughts and feelings, partly for the purpose of becoming more comfortable with sexual thoughts and feelings. We also talked about the kinds of defense systems that people use to handle sexuality. She easily recognized that her intellectual identity was a defense against sexuality. We talked about how people give out signals that either attract or repel others, that these signals rather accurately convey to the opposite sex how comfortable we *really* are with sexuality. She could see, much to her comfort, that this was the probable cause, rather than homosexuality, why she had not been asked out on dates. We discussed the long, but hopeful, process of forming a new identity and how her signals to men would change as she handled her sexual thoughts and feelings more comfortably.

Sometimes adolescents revert to the forms of defense and/or patterns of behavior that they had relied upon in childhood. A co-ed was having a difficult time handling her sexuality and, in addition, she found it difficult to handle the fact that both her parents were being unfaithful. She dressed, talked, and acted like a little girl. After some time she recognized what she was doing and also could talk more openly about what was going on in her family.

Reverting to childhood behavior is not caused solely by fears of sexuality. Other conflicts can also cause this. A co-ed was in her second attempt at college, having failed in her first attempt. After doing well the first term, she suddenly began to do poorly. She cut classes excessively. Just before the final exams for the second term, her corridor mates became alarmed when she stayed in her room and talked baby talk. In the few times I saw her, I sensed that she was trapped in a need to succeed and a need to fail. When the tension between these two poles became too great, she reverted to childhood patterns.

Another girl who had difficulty with sexuality had still another defense. When the tension became too great for her, she would engage in excessive eating. She was raised in a very strict religious tradition in which negative attitudes toward sexuality prevailed. Her emotions ran high both in religion and in sexuality. She had tremendous guilt feelings over sexuality, but managed to develop an appropriate relationship with the opposite sex in spite of these negative feelings. When the conflict between these two positions became too great, however, she would eat excessively.

Less fortunate forms of defense are early marriages and participation in physical heterosexual intimacy at an early age. The former is often an attempt to get out of an unhappy home, an attempt to reject or hurt parents, an attempt to establish early independence, but it also may be an attempt to handle strong sexual impulses. The latter is often an attempt to receive affection and to overcome loneliness. It may also be another form of reverting to infantile methods of obtaining attention and affection, or a way to compensate for the lack of affection in childhood years.

SUMMARY

Because he is entering into an unknown future and solely responsible for himself, the adolescent is a frequent victim of anxiety. It may appear to him that he is about to succumb to chaos. Because he is breaking away from parents and trying out new theories and behavior, the adolescent also lives with a great deal of guilt. It is not easy to retrain the conscience from the infantile to the adult stage. Because the adolescent carries high ideals and evaluates the adult world on the basis of those ideals, he demands the same high level of performance from himself. Although he does not always give this impression to adults, the adolescent is very conscious of his own failings. He experiences a great deal of shame. To be criticized by oneself is often more painful than to be criticized by others. Some adolescents fear they will not become independent from their parents while other adolescents fear that they will not be able to control their emotions. Symptoms such as underachievement and laziness signal other emotional conflicts with which the adolescent is having trouble.

While the most frequent form of defense that adolescents use is sublimation, they also rely upon the safety of the peer group. Here they take advantage of the socialization of guilt, the more tolerant and understanding attitude of their peers, the comfort of their peers in periods of loneliness. In handling their new sex drives, adolescents use a number of defenses, among them an intellectual defense, an ascetic defense, reverting to childhood behavior patterns, and early marriage.

4

DATING

Dating is of recent origin and has received little critical attention. Nevertheless, dating is a sphere in which important adolescent work is accomplished and an activity in which adolescents invest a great deal of time. While dating helps to support the adolescent peer culture and helps young people pass the time enjoyably with each other, dating also poses problems for young people. During their dating years, adolescents must make decisions of far-reaching import. The purpose of this chapter is to explore various dimensions of the dating process.

A Historical Perspective on Dating

Dating as we know it, began at the turn of the century, more exactly, during the 1920's. Prior to this, young people followed the procedure known as "keeping company." Instead of searching far and wide for dating partners and evaluating a host of persons as potential marriage partners, in keeping company, a person dated someone who was known by the family. The partners maintained a high level of commitment to each other, a commitment that usually led to marriage.

The change from the older style of keeping company was part of a more sweeping and complex change in the social order. The change from keeping company to dating was related to the change from the small town to urban society, from a Victorian to a more positive attitude toward sexuality, and from an agrarian to an industrial and technological society. The change to dating was related even more directly to a change in the nature and purpose of marriage and to a new image of woman.

The process leading to marriage in any given society is directly related to the nature and purpose of marriage in that society. In the centuries prior to this one, the emphasis was upon practical rather than personal considerations. Though marriage was not loveless, the major focus of husband and wife was procreation and forming a working team to provide food and shelter for each other and their children. The emphasis was upon what a marriage partner could *do* rather than on what the person was like.[28] It was hoped—indeed, almost expected—that romance would develop between marriage partners. But personal feelings of romance between the two partners *before, or as a condition for, marriage* were not necessary before the 1920's.

If the purpose of marriage had been primarily physical, the purpose came to be primarily emotional. The new social order brought with it a sense of isolation and loneliness. There was growing anonymity. The individual tended to be lost in a mass society. Marriage found a new purpose in meeting the emotional needs of individuals living in this new society. The function of marriage was to secure the personal gratification of the emotional needs of the individual spouses. Romantic love was the ingredient in marriage that would provide the necessary emotions. With intimate interpersonal association as the primary function of marriage, each partner evaluated his mate on the basis of his or her personality, companionability, sexual attractiveness, and the emotional support he or she was able to contribute to the partner. Much less attention was paid to the productive skills of each partner than was paid to his or her sexual and affectional qualities.

Without attempting to establish the line of cause and effect, there was an important change in the image of wife. Instead of being the shy person she was asked to be in the Victorian era, the wife became much more outgoing. Along with her husband, she was entitled to have her emotional and sexual needs met. With an increase in her dignity and worth, she was in a position to choose to whom she was willing to be married. Though she still had to wait for a man to ask her to marry him, and in that sense could not take as much initiative as man, she came a long way toward equality. It was this right to have her personal wishes and needs met which was in contrast with the role she was given in previous centuries.

These two changes, the change in the nature and purpose of marriage and the change in the status and role of women, allowed for, if not called for, a new approach to finding marriage partners.

Dating sprang up spontaneously and was a radical change from keeping company. Instead of choosing from a small circle of persons who were known to the family, young people searched far and wide for partners. Dating lacked the amount of commitment that was entailed in keeping company. In dating, a couple was free from the close scrutiny and supervision of parents, relatives, etc. Instead of relying on the judgment of parents in the selection of a mate, in dating, young people made their own selection. Dating started at a much earlier age than did keeping company. Partly because of the change in attitude toward sex, partly because of the close association of sex with the emotional needs that each partner wished to have met, and partly because of the lack of close supervision, dating entailed a great deal more sexual experimentation over a longer period of time than did keeping company.

The new procedures involved in dating are having a profound effect upon contemporary marriages. There is a carry-over from dating into marriage of the independence and freedom from parents during dating. Upon marriage, couples set up their own home, usually an apartment, and often live many miles from parents. They live an autonomous life, on the one hand, but on the other hand are isolated from parents and relatives, and this contributes to their feelings of anonymity and loneliness. Dating aided persons in handling our more mobile society but also contributed to some of the alleged ailments of our society.

In dating, each partner is evaluated on the basis of the kind of emotional feedback he or she gives the partner. A new standard of evaluation was established. This standard of personal gratification has carried over into marriage and has weakened, if not replaced, the previous standard of dutiful fidelity. Now, even marriage partners are asked to meet that standard, on a continuing basis. For many, the right to personal gratification in marriage has replaced the duty of fidelity.

One of the skills learned in the dating process is the ability to develop and terminate close relationships. Once a person has learned to initiate and break relationships in dating, it is not difficult for him to carry this skill into marriage. If a marriage partner is not suitable according to the new standard, dating has provided the skills necessary to discard one partner and find another, more suitable one.

Finally, just as sex was closely identified with emotional gratification in interpersonal relationships during dating years, so sexual response is very much a part of the emotional gratification that is expected in marriage. This has placed a whole new burden upon sexuality and upon the sexual abilities of marriage partners. The role of sex in dating has carried over into marriage.

The Functions of Dating

Dating is the first, if longest, stage in the process that presently leads to marriage. Courtship is a second stage, during which two persons evaluate each other as possible marriage partners while still engaging in the pattern and functions of dating. If the courtship is successful, it leads to engagement, an even more serious period of evaluation and a time of preparation for marriage. Many of the elements of the dating life-style continue through the engagement period until marriage. Dating may be thought of broadly as this entire time period, or more narrowly, as the initial stage in this process. Marriage, with the level of commitment involved, brings dating to a close.

Dating serves a variety of functions. In dating, the adolescent learns the kind of social poise he needs to attract partners and to live in the adult social world. Dating helps the adolescent test his acceptability in his peer world, particularly among peers of the opposite sex. If successful, his self-esteem is enhanced. Dating helps the adolescent find out what it means to be male or female, as the case may be, and through dating he establishes his sexual identity. He also finds out what those of the opposite sex are like, how to respond to them, and what kinds of responses he elicits from them.

Dating gives young people an opportunity to be exposed to the values, opinions, behavior patterns, hopes, and dreams of other young people, to compare these with those with which they have been raised, and from such a comparison, to develop their own ideas and behavior patterns. Thus dating assists young people in forming their independence and their identity.

Because it is carried on beyond the boundaries of direct parental supervision, dating helps to support the adolescent peer culture. From the peer culture as experienced in dating, the adolescent receives the comfort, understanding, support, and affection that he needs in what may be for him lonely and troubled years. Dating has become the way in which adolescents pass the time among their own, as opposed to the boredom and anxiety they often experience while at home.

Dating offers young people the opportunity to experiment with their own emotional boundaries. As indicated earlier, adolescents feel deeply during these years. In dating they learn to feel deeply toward persons of the opposite sex. Since marriage in contemporary American society is based on romantic love, young people are able to experiment with romance. Adolescents usually experience several crushes. These are prototypes of the romance they will seek in their marriage. These experiences with romance give the adolescent ample opportunity to test his emotional boundaries. Dating, particularly romance, promotes an active imagination. In their imagination young people can anticipate what life will be like with another. In this sense, young people are preparing for marriage. Dating gives the adolescent contact with the opposite sex and therefore he gains experience at various levels of intimacy. In addition, dating allows the adolescent to experiment with commitment. His commitments in dating years are usually of relatively short duration; however, these help to prepare him for the permanency of adult commitments.

Though, in dating, the adolescent is not looking for a marriage partner in any immediate sense, dating does give the adolescent the opportunity to form his ideas about what kind of partner he wishes. In the later dating years there is more of an element of search involved. Since our society relies so heavily on romance as a basis for marriage and since romance can hardly strike without contact with the opposite sex, dating has become a most important phenomenon. Dating is the way a young person puts himself in the market as an eventual marriage partner and the way in which he finds a marriage partner.

Becoming comfortable with his sexual drives, interests, and equipment is another important function of dating. Before elaborating on these functions, however, perhaps it would be wise to describe how the terms "sex" or "sexual" are used in this book. The terms "sex" or "sexual" are used in a broad way, referring to any emotions, feelings, actions that have to do with human sexuality, rather than only in the narrow sense of sexual intercourse. For example, a glance between a young man and a young lady may be a form of sexual expression simply because it is between a male and a female. Kissing is sexual. Sexual intercourse obviously is sexual. All forms and levels of sexual expression, from the broadest to the narrowest, are sexual in the way these terms are used in this book.

Dating in contemporary American society contains a high level of sexual contact and experimentation. To begin with, young people are exposed to sexual stimulation from outside sources. For instance, they are bombarded constantly by mass media and the advertising industry. In addition, the change in sex ethic which began in the 1920's and which has continued intermittently since that time allows for an intense level of sexual experimentation by young people. While technically holding to premarital virginity, American society has nevertheless adopted a system of sexual involvement just short of premarital sex. Any type of sexual play that remains short of full sexual intercourse is, for all practical purposes, allowed. Even this standard seems to be fading steadily in favor of a policy of premarital sexual intercourse with commitment or with affection.[29] Young people become familiar with and learn to handle their own sexual emotions as well as the sexual signals and actions of others. As a result, contemporary young people are much more sophisticated in matters sexual than were young people in earlier generations.

Problems in Dating

Many young people begin dating by the time they reach their mid-teens if not before. Indeed, some parents urge their children to have contact with the opposite sex earlier than this. They arrange for parties where youngsters are paired up for dancing and other activities. While some adolescents may be ready for and wish to date this early, others have little interest in the opposite sex or may not be ready for this level of contact. To these young people dating comes as pressure. They may interpret their lack of interest or their fear negatively, i.e., that something is wrong with them. Or they may feel that they are failing their parents. This is an unfortunate situation and an unnecessary conclusion. Young people differ in their readiness for contact with the opposite sex. There is nothing wrong with the young person who matures more slowly. He should be allowed to set his own pace.

Adolescents have developed a system of relating to the opposite sex that allows for gradually increased levels of intimacy. They have formed different stages of dating as a form of security as they move into the dating process. In preadolescent years, there is a stage that might be called "non-dating." Youngsters become familiar with the opposite sex through contact with other young people in the home and neighborhood. Shortly after puberty, young people begin to look at each other in a new way. Brothers and sisters serve as examples of the opposite sex to each other. Other young people in the neighborhood provide persons with whom to talk and compare notes. Through this informal contact young people begin to relate to the opposite sex.

The second stage is gang dating. A group of boys and girls attend an event or engage in some activity together. Individuals learn to feel comfortable with the opposite sex. They try out procedures of relating to the opposite sex, become familiar with their own feelings as well as the responses they elicit from others. In gang dating, couples may or may not be paired up. There is comfort and security in the group and yet experience at relating to the opposite sex. Even persons who mature late often find a gang-dating situation in which to begin dating.

The next stage is double-dating. Here young people move closer to dating proper. They may invite a person on a double date or an established couple may arrange for such a date. The principle of comfort and security in a group is still in operation. Individuals have the opportunity to relate to a person of the opposite sex on this slightly more intimate level. Finally, dating proper is reached.

As was indicated earlier, dating is the procedure whereby young people make themselves available as potential marriage partners. In this sense, dating leads to marriage. However, dating can mislead partners about each other. In dating, young people attempt to make themselves marketable, i.e., as attractive as possible. Young people do not always get to know the *real* other person. In a dating relationship, each person may have three selves, with the *real* self the hardest to uncover. First, there is "who John really is." Second, there is "who John projects himself to be." Third, there is "the person whom Sally really wants to see in John." This same procedure applies to Sally. Each person projects his best self, and the partner helps that self along through fantasy. It may take a long time for the *real* John and the *real* Sally to meet. Indeed, it may not happen until after they are married. Each partner then may be in for an unhappy surprise. Each partner may feel cheated, even though he or she engaged in the same process. This leads to resentment, retaliation, and unhappiness in marriage. The dating process should, if slowly, reveal each person to the other.

In dating, young people experiment with their emotions. Deep attractions, attachments, and dependencies often form during dating, long before marriage is possible or desirable. When these deep relationships are broken, young people also experience pain very deeply. Our dating process does not protect young people from this pain. Often a dating partner will break a relationship without much of an explanation. The partner may be haunted by such questions as: Why was the relationship broken? What did I do wrong? What is wrong with me? Will I be hurt again? Will anyone ever love me? Often such hurts leave a lasting impression and, instead of experiencing growth from the experience, a young person may surround himself with a defense.

Young people who have gone through such an experience often come to the counseling center. One of the things I discuss with them is that the person who broke the relationship may not be able to explain why. Often the reasons are quite hidden from him. Continuing the relationship, i.e., moving farther into the relationship, with all its implications, may have been too threatening. Any suggestion of, or association with, an increasing level of seriousness may cause a person to break what otherwise was a very happy relationship between two fully acceptable and attractive people.

Not being asked out on dates may cause a person to ask fully as serious questions and draw even more negative conclusions about himself. Though this might appear to apply only to girls, it also applies to boys. If a boy does not receive warm signals from girls, he will not dare to ask a girl out on a date, causing the same negative introspection in him. On occasion a person will come to the counseling center to discuss this situation. I point out that dating is controlled by the signals we give out and, in turn, receive from others. If we give out a warm and positive signal, i.e., a signal that we are ready to have a date and willing to date So-and-So, that message will get through. If, on the other hand, we are hesitant, inexperienced, afraid, etc., that message will be communicated. These signals accurately convey our innermost feelings and, therefore, control the dating process. To correct this problem, a young person can talk about, and therefore work through, the fears and apprehensions he has about himself or about the dating process, and as a consequence begin to give out better signals.

Our system of dating can lead to early marriages, and at present at least, early marriages are proving to be among the most unstable. Dating can lead young people to believe that they are ready for marriage. They have the sexual drives and equipment. They have strong romantic feelings toward each other, the basis for marriage in our society. They can find housing and employment if necessary, though this may be at the expense of continuing their education. Our society does not articulate clearly the fact that it takes more than this to make a marriage work. It is not a coincidence that the age at which people marry has become lower during the same period in which dating has become the accepted method leading to marriage.[30]

An early marriage often means that marriage has taken place before the identities of the two partners are formed. Marriage may have taken place when the identities of the young people were still in an experimental stage. There may be a great amount of change in the identities of each spouse in the early years of marriage. The marriage may or may not be able to handle these changes.

A second feature of early marriage is that one or both spouses may tire of the responsibilities involved in marriage. They may feel that they have missed the freedom and experimentation that other young people, who did not marry early, enjoyed. Resentment against the partner or the children, if there are any, may result. This may lead to the termination of the marriage.

Because our system of dating allows for, if not promotes, a rather high level of sexual experimentation and play during the dating years, certain problems pertaining to sexuality may develop during dating. On the one hand, a young lady may have to develop a variety of techniques to fend off the advances of young men. Yet when she reaches marriage, she must be adept at attracting her husband and skilled in her sexual performance. Fending off advances is not good training for full and free expression of her sexuality in marriage. And the warnings that her parents may give about "men" in her dating years, in order to make sure that she does resist advances, can sometimes do irreparable damage to a young lady.

In our system, an adolescent may engage in intimate forms of sexual play at an early age. This may have rather unfortunate results. The young person may form a fixation on sexuality and may rely almost exclusively upon sex as a means of responding to partners. Intense sexual involvement at an early age is a risk. Intimacy with the opposite sex is something that is handled with greater ease in the late teens. Early experimentation with sex may disturb the ability to respond as a total person. It may cause a fixation on simple genitality, on mere physical sex, rather than on a more total form of intimacy, i.e., the meeting of two whole persons. Young people, particularly girls, may be drawn into such a behavior pattern if they believe that sex will get them dates. Such behavior deters the maturation of the total person. Such a response may *seem* appropriate at the moment. However, after marriage, if not before, this response will prove too limited. A marriage partner wishes more in a relationship than sexual response, as important as that is. The young person should develop his whole person in dating.

It is difficult to find an appropriate level of sexual activity before marriage. If there is little or no contact before marriage, the expectation of sexual activity in marriage may run extremely high. Marriage may not be able to deliver that much. Or, little contact may indicate a fear of sexual activity. This may leave a person ill prepared for the intimacy involved in marriage. On the other hand, a great deal of sexual play before marriage may cause a fixation on physical sex or may leave little to anticipate in marriage. Marriage may turn out to be a bore. Young people have a difficult task in finding a balanced approach to premarital sexual activity.

Conflicting Values and Myths

The moratorium that is offered to youth in adolescence is not total. During the dating years there are some important decisions that young people face. Among these are decisions between conflicting values held within our society. In addition, adolescents may face a conflict between a theory held by society and practices in our society that conflict with this theory. The decisions that young people make will help to determine the kind of persons they will be, the type of marriage they will have, and the kind of world in which they will live. Let us look at some of these conflicting areas.

On the one hand, each adolescent wishes to be a unique individual with his own personality. This is one of the key values of the adolescent. On the other hand, there are forces at work in society, to which each adolescent is vulnerable, which tend to undermine individuality and uniqueness. For its own economic purposes, the advertising industry has developed an image of "girl" and is having increasing success in forming an image of "young man" as well. Adolescents are led to believe that if they look and act like these images, they will enjoy the success that advertising portrays these images as having. Young people (older people as well) are drawn toward conforming to these images.

The image that a young person projects to a member of the opposite sex is very important in dating years. Each person tries to project an image that will be interesting and will result in a date. It is very easy under these circumstances for adolescents to adopt the image of "girl" and "young man." Yet the young person who succumbs to these images gives up his chance to be a unique self. And conformity leads to anonymity. He may gain acceptance with his peers, but he will lose his opportunity to be a unique person. There is insight into this problem in the comment made by a young man about girls who are controlled by the image of "girl." "When you've dated one," he said, "you've dated them all." When young people accept these images, they put themselves in a situation where each person can be replaced by another. Relationships between persons who have accepted these images are liable to be shallow because each person is really only a type or representative. Encounter between two types is far different from encounter between two unique persons. Further, any person who accepts one of these images does not inspire responsibility in his dating companion. He is liable to be treated as an object, as a thing, and exploited. Conversely, being a unique person tends to inspire respect and responsibility in dating partners.

Young people also face a conflict between using their reason or following their feelings. Mass media, in particular the TV and movie industries, urge young people to follow their natural feelings. Because these feelings come from deep inside the individual, they must be right. In a movie I saw recently, the leading man was urged by the seductress: "Don't think about it; feelings are much more human." With the arrival of this position, the pendulum has swung to the opposite pole from where it had been. For centuries, feelings and emotions were distrusted. This position was as unwarranted and unfortunate as this new position. To be human means to have and use both mind and body, the faculties of reason and emotion. Following only reason or only intellect, young people will experience only a distortion of human life.

Young people face decisions over still another point of view promulgated by the advertising industry. This is the myth that sex is power. Evidently the advertising industry has found that sex sells products. Girls are draped over automobiles. They run their fingers sexily over stoves and refrigerators. In addition, the advertising industry attempts to sell the myth that by using specific products, an individual will become more attractive and will have success in falling in love, etc., etc. Both of these positions give the public the notion that sex is a tool that will help us acquire those things which we wish to have. Young people are particularly vulnerable as they work on being accepted by members of the opposite sex. A judge working with a divorce court recently bemoaned the results in girls: "They're brought up to think that all they need is their femaleness, which often turns out to be helplessness, hesitancy, and indecisiveness." Instead of a means of deep communication between two people, sex becomes a gimmick. The result is a fixation on sex to the exclusion of the development of other dimensions of the personality. The temptation, however, is great.

What Kind of Person? What Kind of World?

An adolescent is in a state of transition from childhood to adulthood. This fact has important implications in the area of ethics. During childhood, authority and a system of ethics were provided by parents, community, and the church. To be an adult, a person must develop his own *internal* authority and his own system of ethics. While the person was a child, he was cared for. As an adult, the person cares for himself and for the world in which he lives. The adult is responsible for the kind of person he is and the kind of world in which he lives. During adolescence, the young person must move from a childlike to an adult stance in life.

In the early years of adolescence, the young person is trying to free himself from external authority. Often he simply takes positions or engages in behavior the opposite of what his parents or society hold. In this way he develops his autonomy, his ability to stand alone, and his self-confidence. But this is only the first stage in the move toward adulthood. During the second stage of adolescence, the young person must move toward a position that entails more responsibility than simple conformity to parental positions or reaction against them. He must move to a position where he takes responsibility for himself and for the world in which he lives.

Already in his dating years, simple conformity or reaction will not suffice. The adolescent is faced with problems and decisions that affect the kind of person he will be and the kind of world in which he will live. He must gather the opinions of others and must study the philosophy of life and system of ethics of others, including those of his parents, community, and church. Instead of asking what position he must take in order to assert his independence, he must ask what kind of person he wishes to be and what kind of world he wishes to have. When he approaches life with such questions, he will be taking the stance of the adult. It is hoped that he will begin to take such a stance toward the decisions he faces in dating. If he is to be responsible, the adolescent cannot rely on either the argument "My parents said" or on the argument "Everyone is doing it." Both positions are relying on external authority. The adult is responsible for himself and his world. The adolescent must move in the direction of this kind of responsibility.

SUMMARY

Dating developed spontaneously early in the twentieth century as a part of the changing social scene in America. It is closely related to the new nature and purpose of marriage.

Dating serves a variety of functions. Through dating, a young person learns social poise, gains confidence, and develops his sexual identity. In dating, young people compare values, opinions, etc., with their peers and begin to develop their own points of view. Dating offers youth the opportunity to experiment with their emotional boundaries and to respond to the opposite sex. In more serious forms of dating, young people make themselves marketable for marriage and search for a marriage partner.

Young people face problems in dating. They must handle the pressure to date. A young person must learn to sort through the images that his partner projects and at-

tempt to find out and evaluate the *real* person. Broken
relationships can be very painful to young people. Having
no dates at all can be equally painful. Dating may lead a
person to marry before he is ready for the responsibility
entailed in marriage. A much more open attitude toward
sexuality means that young people must be prepared to
handle a high level of sexual experimentation during their
dating years. Young people must also make decisions over
conflicting values and myths.

In deciding on what positions to take on the issues he
faces, the adolescent cannot rely on either simple conformity or reaction. Rather, he must move in the direction
of adult responsibility and make decisions on the basis
of the kind of person he wishes to be and the kind of world
he wishes to have.

5

DEVELOPING
A SEX ETHIC

Sex is an area where young people face decisions. There is no moratorium in sex. During their adolescent years, young people must form their attitude toward sex and choose a sex ethic, i.e., the moral guidelines that they will follow. This is a formidable task for contemporary young people because we are currently in the middle of a sexual revolution. Developing a sex ethic in a period of far-reaching social change is difficult.

Normally there is a consensus within a society over values and standards. The entire society helps to uphold the values and standards that it holds. In this situation it is clear to young people what the values and standards are. This is not the situation in our society. Presently we are looking for a new value system and new rules regarding sex.

This situation presents somewhat of a confusing climate for youth. On the one hand, they feel the weight of earlier rules, and on the other hand, they must search for new guidelines. In this situation more responsibility for finding an acceptable and workable standard is placed on the individual. Instead of being guided by the consensus of society, young people must decide somewhat on an individual basis the kind of persons they wish to be and the kind of world they wish to have.[31]

This is not to say, however, that sexual behavior is guided solely, or even mostly, by ethical systems. It is not. Probably more than any sex ethic, sexual behavior is determined by peer behavior. This is true of the sexual behavior of contemporary young people. Nevertheless, a sex ethic does play a role within society.

This chapter has a twofold purpose: first, to describe and contrast three sex moralities and, second, to give young people a picture of the changing assumptions, values, and rules of the past and to describe some of the features of the current sexual revolution. It is hoped that young people will find an acceptable morality among those offered as well as gain a perspective on the sexual scene from the historical sketch and from the description of current developments. There is little doubt that peer culture is the most influential force in determining the sexual attitudes and behavior of youth. Perhaps, however, the content of this chapter can become an additional dimension of the total climate on which youth draw as they relate to one another sexually.

Comparative Moralities

The traditional sex ethic holds that sexual intercourse should be reserved for marriage. By making marriage the standard for sexual intercourse, the adherents of the traditional approach were attempting to protect society and the individual partners. Since sexual intercourse might lead to procreation, for the protection of the child and the welfare of society there should be the *maturity* and the *level of commitment* assumed in marriage. Second, since at its best, sexual intercourse involves two people sharing their deepest feelings, each partner should have the pledge of *lifetime commitment.* Only with that level of commitment can sexual intercourse fulfill its potential. Another principle involved in the traditional approach is that marriage is a public act and therefore provides a well-defined boundary line for people to follow. It provides a rule clear enough to follow and enforce.

A number of new attempts at developing a sex ethic have been made recently. Because of their similarity they will be discussed together. Together they comprise a sex ethic that rivals the traditional approach. Joseph Fletcher, in a system that is called "situation ethics," shies away from the kind of hard-and-fast rule involved in the traditional approach. Fletcher holds that no law can cover the variety of situations that actually exist. Each situation must be evaluated on its own merit.

A standard of evaluation is offered by Lester Kirkendall. Rather than drawing the lines of sexual morality on the basis of abstinence from premarital intercourse, Kirkendall holds that *the quality of the interpersonal relationship* should be the determining factor.

> Morality does not reside in complete sexual abstinence, nor immorality in having had nonmarital experience. Rather, sex derives its meaning from the extent to which it contributes to or detracts from the quality and meaning of the relationship in which it occurs, and relationships in general.[32]

Kirkendall holds that to be moral, behavior should create trust, confidence, integrity, and self-respect. Conversely, acts that create distrust, suspicion, misunderstanding, and build barriers between people are immoral.

Closely associated with the positions of Fletcher and Kirkendall is the position of John A. T. Robinson called the "new morality." In the new morality, *love* is the standard by which people are to be guided, rather than the boundary line of marriage. Love is defined here in the sense of the Biblical word *agapē,* concern about and care for the other person.

Another approach to sexual morality is offered by Vance Packard.[33] Packard's position is very close to the traditional sex ethic. Packard would draw the line of morality on the basis of *the couple's maturity and level of commitment as evidenced by the public announcement of engagement,* rather than the actual marriage ceremony. Because engagement indicates a pledge to marry, and therefore a high level of maturity as well as commitment, both society and the individual partners are protected. This approach is based on the assumption that birth control aids would be available to couples during engagement. With the intention to marry shortly, and with birth control techniques, the couple would be allowed to engage in physical union if they so desired. Holding the same values as does the traditional approach, Packard has simply moved the line of morality to a slightly earlier point.

There are some important areas of agreement between these various approaches. All the systems mentioned above reject a position of complete sexual freedom. No matter how "private" the sex act may seem, it has social implications. To be acceptable, a moral standard must be as concerned with the public good as it is with personal pleasure, even if that be between consenting adults. Each of the systems above outlaws the exploitation of an individual for personal sexual satisfaction. Any system that leaves one partner in shame, uncertain, or degraded is unacceptable. A view that is growing in popularity, described as "permissive with affection," also is unacceptable, if affection refers to the kind of casual affection that young people express throughout their dating years. Affection does not guarantee a meaningful sex act. These systems also find unacceptable sexual union that is dominated only by physical urges. This is only a fraction of what sexual intercourse is meant to be. There is great danger that future sexual encounters will run no more deeply than physical expression. A sexual act that is used to demonstrate one's masculinity or femininity also falls below the standards required.

Finally, though they do not expressly say so, all three of the above ethical systems require a certain level of emotional maturity in both partners before sexual intercourse can be considered morally acceptable. By tying sexual intercourse to marriage, the traditional approach was assuming such maturity. Vance Packard expressly states it as a requirement. And I believe that the moral systems outlined by Fletcher, Kirkendall, and Robinson, though they could be much clearer on this point, also require emotional maturity as a moral prerequisite. This point has not been made to young people as clearly as it should have been. Until a person's identity is fully formed, he runs a risk in intimate sexual contacts. Erik Erikson points out that there is an indeterminate gap between the development of sexual urges at puberty and the time in later adolescence or early adulthood when the young person is able to handle intimacy constructively.[34] Intimacy before identity is set may cause one's boundaries to become fuzzy and cause fear in the person. Early physical intimacy, before emotional maturity is reached, may cause a fixation on the physical dimensions of sexuality. Later this may be the only dimension of sex that a person is capable of giving and receiving. We become ready for intimacy in late adolescence and early adulthood. Packard is quite right in emphasizing emotional maturity as one of the criteria for a moral standard.

Each of these approaches to sexual morality has advantages and disadvantages which should be considered. One of the advantages of the traditional standard is that it provides a recognizable boundary for sexual intercourse for individuals and for society. A second advantage, one not to be considered lightly, is that it assumes the necessary level of maturity and commitment. Again, the individuals and society are protected by this rule. By ruling out sexual intercourse until marriage, the traditional standard keeps young people from focusing too narrowly on sex. Instead it promotes the growth of the total person. The fact that the traditional approach contains an ideal for society and for youth is an additional advantage. An ideal, if it is not beyond the reach of too many people, gives society as a whole a goal to shoot for. It gives the society character and it gives self-esteem to individuals.

The traditional standard has some disadvantages. Perhaps the first disadvantage is its association with a negative and repressive attitude toward sex. Though the traditional standard need not be tied to a negative view of sex, nevertheless, in the minds of many people, this association is made. In an age that has recently broken with that attitude toward sex, the traditional standard does not receive much of a hearing. Because it is ignored by a large segment of our population, it is not a very viable option for young people. Second, the traditional standard does not concern itself directly with the quality of the relationship between two people; rather, it assumes that quality will be present if the standard is kept. This assumption is somewhat unrealistic. The traditional standard seems more interested in establishing a boundary than it is in establishing quality relationships.

A third disadvantage of the traditional standard is that it is unable to respond to change. Indeed, it acts as if nothing changes. For instance, it was inaugurated in a time when people knew little about contraception. It sought to protect society by assuring a family setting for any child who was born. Now, however, there are contraceptive devices that can give that same assurance to society, yet the standard stays the same. The traditional standard is also insensitive to differing conditions. For instance, in Biblical times, young people were married soon after puberty. It is a different thing to hold to the traditional standard in that situation than in our present situation, when young people must go through long years of schooling while, at the same time, they are bombarded with sexual stimuli.

The "wait until marriage" approach can cause some difficulties. The standard may place a burden of lifelong guilt on those who are unable to wait. This standard, at least in the past, came down very hard on those who failed to live up to the ideal. In this sense also, the traditional standard seems more interested in maintaining a legalistic standard than in developing quality relationships. Finally, rather than allowing a couple to follow their own pace toward sexual fulfillment, it establishes one right moment.

The system of morality proposed by Fletcher, Kirkendall, and Robinson has some advantages. In contrast to the traditional standard, it focuses on *the quality of the relationship*. Rather than responding to a rule, the individuals have as their goal establishing a quality relation-

ship. They decide whether or not to have sexual intercourse on the basis of whether or not sexual intercourse
would help or hinder the relationship. *The relationship is
more important than the rule.* A second advantage of this
approach is that it is flexible. This approach is sensitive to
changing times and conditions; it is also sensitive to the
fact that the line of morality is different in different situations. Third, this standard seems to put less attention on
the goodness or badness of persons based on whether or
not they have kept a rule and therefore it creates less guilt
in the general populace. Finally, this approach takes some
of the emphasis off sex. Whether or not a person has engaged or is engaging in premarital sexual intercourse is not
the critical thing. People are thus freed to respond to each
other in additional ways. This approach serves to de-em-
phasize sex.

This system of morality also has some disadvantages.
First, there is no clear moral standard for the populace.
This leaves youth confused as to what is expected of them.
Second, this approach is not so clear as it could be over
who should come under this system of morality. It is
doubtful whether persons of all ages are mature enough
to handle this approach. Third, it is a "private" ethic. And
even when the problem of conception is handled by contraceptives, society still has a stake in the type of relationships that develop among the citizenry. No human act is
really private. The nature of society is always at stake.
Fourth, in this approach each couple has to decide whether
or not the relationship will be enhanced and whether the
act is being governed by love. This assumes a great deal
more rationality in the decision-making process than
actually is present, especially in a society that is dominated
by the romantic love myth. Young people in late adoles-

cence are particularly vulnerable to this approach. They have all the marks of maturity and responsibility. They experience what may be called "pseudo-adulthood." They may easily be led to believe that what they are experiencing is "for real" when in actuality it is only a semblance of adulthood. This approach gives few guidelines as to what constitutes maturity, nor does it define what constitutes a quality relationship. Instead it operates on the basis of the feelings of the two persons involved. This approach is fuzzy in the amount of commitment that there should be in a relationship that involves sexual intercourse. If the proponents of this system are serious about having love as the standard, it is more idealistic, and perhaps unrealistic, than the traditional standard.

The morality system that Vance Packard proposes has many of the advantages listed under the traditional standard. By changing the standard from marriage to engagement, Packard has kept a recognizable boundary. An advantageous level of maturity and of commitment are also demanded. Society and the individuals are protected. By ruling out sexual intercourse before engagement, this approach keeps young people from focusing early and too narrowly on sex. It also protects young people from being lured into sexual intimacy by feelings that have all the earmarks of love but that are not supported by commitment. This approach holds out an ideal, one that is realistic and workable.

Going beyond the advantages that it shares with the traditional approach, Packard's standard conveys the notion of understanding and flexibility. It conveys a positive attitude toward sex and understanding of the sexual pressures on young people. It recognizes that there have been changes, particularly in the area of birth control, and that as a result, an adjustment can be made in the moral standard. Society and the individuals remain protected. By drawing the line somewhere *during* engagement, Packard is allowing the couple to establish their own pace toward sexual intimacy. There is no exact line that makes the act moral or immoral. Within the boundaries of engagement, with the level of maturity and commitment which that entails, the quality of the relationship becomes the determining factor.

One of the disadvantages of a system that tries to steer a middle course is that it may please few. Those who hold to the traditional standard may ask if there is no one *right* position and those who wish to be guided by the situation may feel that Packard's approach is still too rigid. Though there may be approximately the same level of maturity, or nearly so, in persons at the time of engagement as there is at marriage, the level of commitment entailed in engagement is less than in marriage. Therefore, Packard has settled for less commitment than is involved in the traditional standard. Finally, just as there were situations to which the traditional standard could not respond, so there may be situations to which the standard of engagement may not respond. In this sense persons are still responding to a rule rather than to a situation.

Young people have available to them a variety of approaches to sexual morality. Each young person will have to decide for himself which sex ethic he will follow.

A Historical Perspective

Young people may be helped in the task of choosing a sex ethic if they are aware of the assumptions, values, and rules that prevailed in the past. Since the church was the main source of these in the Western world, outside the influence that the environment has always had, the discussion will center on the assumptions, values, and rules about sex held by the church.

While the church remained on Palestinian soil, she built upon the attitudes toward sex that prevailed among the Hebrews. The Hebrews had a positive view of sex. They assumed that the world was the creation of a good and loving God and that sexuality was a part of God's creation. Except where sex might disrupt family life, and therefore society, the Hebrews allowed sex rather free expression. The Hebrews were concerned about protecting their society. They believed that they had an important role to play in the world. They were the standard-bearers for God. In order to fulfill this national purpose, they sought to protect their society from disruption. The family was one of the major institutions in their society and therefore they protected it. However, as long as sexuality did not jeopardize the family, it was allowed free expression.

When the church moved from Palestinian soil to the Greco-Roman world, her attitude toward sex changed radically. The church came to have a very negative view of sex. There were two reasons for this change, both having to do with the new environment. First, the church saw sexual attitudes and practices in the Greco-Roman world that were very disruptive of society and potentially dangerous for the church. Since the church felt that she had

taken over from Judaism the role of being the standard-
bearer for God, the church had the same interest in maintaining a stable society that the Hebrews had.

Among the attitudes and practices that the church found
threatening was the view of woman which prevailed. In the
Greco-Roman world the role of wife was a lowly one. Her
place was in the home managing the household and caring
for her children. She was duty-bound, cloistered, and
mentally circumscribed. She was not considered a fitting
intellectual or sexual partner for her husband. There were
other women who served these "loftier" functions. In contrast to women, men were free to roam at will throughout
the community, engaging in work, discussion, and enter-
tainment. There was a dual sexual standard. Men might
philander at will, but if a wife was caught in adultery, she
could be punished severely.

In this climate, marriage was unpopular. The population sank to such a low level that the great lawmaker,
Solon, attempted to make marriage compulsory. Unfaith-
fulness rather than fidelity characterized marriage. Someone else's wife always seemed more exciting. Sexual intercourse was purely an activity for personal sensual pleasure.
In this situation the family deteriorated. Women did not
want the obligation of children. Contraception and abortion were the order of the day among the well-to-do, while
abandoning infants was the practice of the poorer people.
Divorce was rampant. Though technically illegal, adultery
was commonplace. This environment startled the church
and threatened her values.

The second reason why the church developed a negative
attitude toward sex was that she adopted the dualistic
view of life that prevailed in the Greco-Roman world. In

this dualistic view, the mental or spiritual world is good while the material or physical world is evil. The church began to look with disdain upon sex. Indeed the church turned its wrath upon sex.

To cope with the excesses in Greco-Roman society, and to curb man's sexual drive, the church drew upon Stoicism, which was a prevalent philosophy at the time. First, the church adopted the idea that there was an overarching natural law by which all human behavior was to be governed. Second, man's life should be under the control of reason. Man's emotions rose out of his physical nature while his reason emanated from the spiritual world. Third, all human activity had to serve some rational purpose. Fourth, the purpose of sexuality was procreation.

From these assumptions the church developed her values and rules regarding sex. Since the sex act was physical, the nonsexual life of virginity or celibacy was considered a better life. Virginity and celibacy came to be held in higher esteem than marriage. Because the sexual act involved, if only for a moment, emotion over reason, it was considered a sinful act. To carry out her destiny, however, the church had to procreate and educate. Much to the church's embarrassment, procreation involved sexuality. On the other hand, procreation gave purpose to sexuality, thus legitimizing sexual intercourse. The church established the rules that the *only* purpose of sexual intercourse was procreation. Personal pleasure was not a legitimate reason for sexual intercourse.

Since the purpose of sexual intercourse was procreation, the church drew up the rule that any act which undercut that purpose was wrong. Thus, any form of contraception was wrong, as was abortion. And since masturbation involved only personal pleasure and could not, by its very nature, cause procreation, it was considered a particularly evil act.

The church's attitude toward marriage was ambiguous. On the one hand, marriage was believed to be ordained by God and therefore was good. It was the proper way to pursue procreation. The family was one of the means of education; it helped the church pursue her mission. On the other hand, marriage involved sexuality, and since that was evil, virginity and celibacy were higher styles of living than was marriage. Since sexual intercourse, and therefore conception, involved emotion, it was sinful. Since all children were born in a sinful act, all children were born in sin and carried the taint of sin. This idea, which took doctrinal form, did not enhance the vocation of marriage and family life.

What is particularly regrettable about the assumptions, values, and rules that developed in this environment is that they went unquestioned for approximately twelve centuries. This helps to account for the powerful negative influence the church has had upon sexuality.

A break in this system of assumptions, values, and rules first appeared in the thirteenth century with Thomas Aquinas. Aquinas held that pleasure, as such, was neither good nor bad. Nor was pleasure particularly contrary to reason, though an *excess* of pleasure was contrary to reason. An increasing number of people held that, since according to nature not all sexual intercourse leads to procreation, not all sexual intercourse need be engaged in solely for the purpose of procreation. Further, a growing number of people held that man's sexual urges were "natural" and therefore should be accepted. Nature was still the guideline; however, this time the argument of nature was running counter to the former dualistic view of the world and toward a more positive view of the physical world, including sexuality.

The Renaissance and the Reformation, with the accompanying rise of the middle class, brought still further changes, and, of course, a division in the church. Of no small importance was the rise of the notion of democracy, i.e., that the wisdom of the many is as authoritative, if not more authoritative, than the wisdom of the few. This had profound implications for the authority and structure of the church. Because Luther had a more positive attitude toward sexuality than the church had had earlier, he called into question the view that celibacy and virginity were higher forms of life than marriage. Luther gave marriage a boost. Calvin shared this higher view of sex and struck a blow at the low estimate of woman that the church had held. Calvin saw woman's primary role as companion of man. Her role of child bearing and rearing was secondary. This also gave marriage a new footing. Marriage was for companionship; procreation was secondary. Sex was seen as one means of expressing affection between husband and wife. In this new age and environment, the church was able to hold to a more positive attitude toward sex and still feel confident that she could fulfill her mission in the world.

By the eighteenth century, the changes that had been emerging since the thirteenth century were forming a lifestyle radically different from that of the early centuries. Sex was viewed positively, and its legitimate expression valued. In the Protestant branch of the church, Scriptural authority and the will of the majority were the guiding standards. The spell of reason over emotion was broken, although a certain amount of distrust of emotion lingered in the church and in Western society. A more wholistic view of the created order began to replace the dualistic picture which the church had borrowed. Though the concept of purpose remained a strong motif in both branches of the church, the purpose of sexual intercourse was broadened to include affection and pleasure, in addition to procreation. It should be pointed out, however, that these many centuries of a negative view of sex could not easily be erased from the minds of people living in the Western world.

That memory was stimulated by the Victorian era. During this era prudishness and shame about sex prevailed. Whereas earlier Puritans had called things by their real names, these later Puritans developed words and phrases to use in place of words and phrases that had sexual overtones. Clothing styles helped to carry out this prudishness. Long dresses, purposely hooped away from the body, helped women appear as though they had no legs—as did the way they learned to walk. When women went to the doctor, they pointed to a doll to indicate where they were having difficulty. Bathroom functions were draped in secrecy. The image of woman was shy, delicate, motherly, and passive. She was not to have any sexual urges. Sexual intercourse, though not thought to be sinful, was thought to be dirty. The shame of sexuality was communicated to children through silence about sex or by labeling it "dirty."

The Victorian era was a reaction to a period of rationalism which had preceded it, and in that sense it was a change brought about by a new cultural climate. In the Victorian era there was a highly emotional, albeit negative, fixation on sex. The Victorian era brought a new emphasis on sex, and at the same time a denial of sex. It was a rearrangement of assumptions and values of the past.

Its impact on the general populace, however, was that of a negative and prudish view of sex.

The Sexual Revolution

The twentieth century has brought a whole new sexual scene. Many of the assumptions, values, and rules have been questioned. Some have been discarded; and it appears that more changes may still be coming. One fact of no small significance in this situation is the loss of influence of the church. The populace has tended to go its own way. The church has been caught with allegiance to, or has been associated with, the assumptions, values, and rules of the past, while the general populace has ignored many of these traditions.

The twentieth century has seen a move toward a more positive and wholesome view of sex. Indeed, there is some reason to believe that the general populace, if not the church, has swung with the proverbial pendulum to a point of uncritical indulgence in sex. In both Roman Catholic and Protestant branches of the church, there has been a flurry of scholarship supporting a positive attitude toward sexuality. Indeed, few churchmen now wish to play the role of critic.

One new assumption that has come to have wide acceptance in this century is the equality of the sexes. Though this principle had been developing over the centuries, it is reaching new dimensions in this century. This position is in stark contrast to the view of woman that was held by the early church. One implication of this new assumption is the resexualization of women. In contrast to the Victorian era, now women are allowed to express their sexual feelings and to have their sexual needs met. A second result is a change in the image of both male and female in Western society, with less polarity between the sexes.

Another new fact of our time is the desacralization of sex. Sex is no longer the mystery it once was. Now man can be guided by medical science and technology rather than by "natural law." Man's sexuality is being studied clinically. His emotional and physical responses are being scrutinized carefully. The subject of sex is taught to all age groups in many schools and churches. Medical science has increased our knowledge about sex and has given us reliable methods of contraception and safe methods of abortion. The sex education movement has also brought a whole new attitude toward masturbation, replacing the repressive and frightening approaches of the past.

Even though both branches of the church had abandoned procreation as the primary purpose of marriage, the rules about contraception and abortion, which grew out of that earlier position, remained. The populace of the Western world has been putting pressure on the church to change her attitude toward contraception, if not abortion. Early in the century, the Roman Catholic Church gave in to that pressure to the extent that she would permit a "natural" form of contraception, the rhythm method. The Protestant branch of the church went farther and allowed contraception, using various techniques. There continues to be a great deal of pressure on the Roman Catholic hierarchy to change the rule on contraception, if not abortion. Meanwhile, the populace has turned en masse to the use of contraceptives, and state legislatures are taking it upon themselves to change abortion laws. The Roman Catholic Church is also under heavy pressure to change her attitudes and rules regarding celibacy and virginity and to bring these into line with the positive view she now has toward sex and marriage.

The twentieth century has seen civilization reach a new problem, that of overpopulation. Whereas before, civilization always faced the threat of underpopulation, now overpopulation is a problem. In the past, the church feared underpopulation because of her mission. Because of this she promoted marriage, procreation, and the family. The question is whether the church can rethink and rearrange her values in the light of this important new fact. This is an example of how changed conditions cause man to rethink his system of morality from his assumptions all the way to his rules.

One of the most significant developments of the twentieth century has been the change in attitude and behavior regarding premarital sexual intercourse. Until the twentieth century, the rule regarding sexual intercourse was that it was to be confined to marriage. During this century, beginning in the 1920's, there has been an increase in the acceptance of, and participation in, premarital sexual intercourse. In the most recent years, the rate of participation in premarital sexual intercourse by women has been catching up with men.[35] In addition, there has been widespread participation in petting during dating and courtship years. Together, this has amounted to a new pattern of sexual behavior before marriage.

There are many reasons why this change has occurred, among them the loss of influence by the church, increasing disregard for norms externally imposed, the spontaneous response of young people to heightened sexual stimulation, better techniques and wider acceptance of contraception, control over venereal disease by medicine, the mobility and privacy that the automobile offers young people, the search for affection in an age of growing anonymity, and a reaction against the prudishness of the Victorian era. But deeper than these, society is questioning some of the assumptions and values that have been held for centuries.

First, sexual behavior has come to be seen more as a private act, to be judged by private standards rather than as a public act which society should control. There is an increasing emphasis on the right of the individual to pursue his own personal pleasure rather than always thinking of the good of society, especially if, through the use of contraceptives, he protects society from procreation. In short, there is more focus on personal pleasure than on concern for society's well-being. The assumption that premarital sex will injure society, an assumption held for many centuries, is being questioned. Perhaps the loss of the feeling of destiny or purpose by the church and/or society accounts for this reversal in values.

Second, the rule that sexual intercourse must be confined to marriage is being questioned. The level of commitment that society earlier had thought necessary for the welfare of the individuals is being questioned. People are settling for lesser levels of commitment, short of that involved in marriage. It is now held by some that premarital sex can be enjoyed without harm to individuals; therefore, sexual intercourse need not be confined to marriage. In addition, there are those who have come to hold that sex does not have to be tied to commitment at all, but that sexual intercourse may be simply a form of giving and receiving affection between two individuals who wish it.

In moving all the way from seeing procreation as the only legitimate reason for sexual intercourse to seeing it as a means of giving and receiving affection between individuals, society has moved from judging the act on the basis of society's welfare to the personal pleasure of individuals. Clearly values have changed!

Just where contemporary society will settle on the issues it is now discussing remains to be seen. In its early centuries, the church believed that sex had devious power. The current assumption of mass media is that sex has magical powers. It remains to be seen what estimate the general public will come to on this broad spectrum. Currently the church holds the position that sex is meant to enhance the marital relationship. Other members of society believe that sex need not be confined to that purpose but can be seen in a much more playful sense. Just what role society will assign sex in the future remains uncertain. In the past the church held that sexual intercourse outside marriage was detrimental to society and to the individuals involved. An increasing number of persons in our society reject this assumption. There is evidence that under some conditions, persons have reported no ill effects; others reported that there were benefits. There were also some who reported ill effects.[36] Where the boundary line will eventually be placed, guarding those who are emotionally too immature for this level of intimacy, as well as establishing a required level of affection or commitment, remains to be seen.

Attitudes and rules from the past tend to linger and are joined by more recent attitudes and rules to create quite a confusing picture. It is hoped that this sketch of attitudes and rules, past and present, will help young people in the decision-making process which they face.

SUMMARY AND CONCLUSIONS

Three sexual moralities were described and compared: the traditional standard, which holds that sexual intercourse should be reserved for marriage; the "new morality" approach, which focuses on the quality of the interpersonal relationship and requires that the decision over sexual intercourse before marriage be based on the Christian concept of love; and a standard proposed by Vance Packard, that engagement marks a sufficiently high level of emotional maturity and commitment to allow a couple to engage in sexual intercourse if they so choose. Each of these approaches has its pros and cons which young people will have to weigh carefully.

Though the church inherited a positive view of sex from the Hebrews, when she moved to the Greco-Roman world the church adopted a negative view of sex. This negative view of sex went unquestioned for twelve centuries. Indeed, many of the attitudes and the rules that developed in this negative era have lingered. Since the time of Aquinas, the church has slowly recovered a positive view of sex. The purpose of sexual intercourse has broadened to include personal pleasure. Women have come to be held in higher esteem, as has marriage. A loss in the authority of the church and the rise of the middle class has helped to bring about a break with some of the old assumptions, values, and rules relating to sex.

In this century we are experiencing a sexual revolution. Additional assumptions, values, and rules about sex are being questioned, and the end of this questioning is not in sight. Finding a meaningful and workable sex ethic in all this confusion is difficult. Obviously, young people will be influenced by their peers. It is hoped, however, that young people will find this critique of contrasting sex moralities and this sketch of changing assumptions, values, and rules helpful as they attempt to develop a sex ethic for themselves.

6

DEVELOPING SELF-ESTEEM

In seeing a chapter devoted to the subject of self-esteem, the reader should not conclude that inferiority feelings are the unique problem of the adolescent. They are not. Children and adults alike suffer from low self-esteem. Two reasons prompt the inclusion of this chapter. First, during adolescence the young person gains a perspective on his past which, because of the lack of intellectual maturity, he did not have before. The adolescent is in a very reflective and introspective mood, thinking through his past, mulling over the impact of his childhood experiences, and to some extent, breaking some of his ties with the past. Second, precisely because the adolescent is able to gain a new perspective on his past and because he is in the process of establishing his own identity, he is able to *do something about* his self-image. He has the opportunity to gain a new perspective on his past, draw new conclusions about himself, and therefore live by more appropriate and suitable hypotheses about himself and his world. In this sense, adolescence is a time of hope. This is not to say that there are no risks in adolescence. There are. Just as self-esteem may improve, so also it may deteriorate. The adolescent years may contribute to low self-esteem. Nevertheless, for the most part, adolescence provides the young person with the opportunity to reevaluate his childhood self-image and experiences, and with his new intellectual power, draw new and more positive conclusions about himself. It is hoped that this chapter will aid this process in young people.

The Genesis of Inferiority Feelings

The conditions that cause the development of inferiority feelings within a person are many and varied. For the most part, such feelings have their origin in the early years of childhood. However, they may receive support and confirmation in later childhood and adolescent years. We will look at both periods.

The estimate that a person has of himself is determined largely through interpersonal relationships. Everyone must feel significant in the eyes of some other person or persons. That significance comes from the quality of the relationship that develops between the self and others. It should also be understood that a person's self-estimate is the result of the interpretation he makes of his relationship with others. In other words, what matters to the person is not what others actually think, but *what he thinks they think of him.*

Since an individual's early experiences in life determine how he feels about himself as well as how he views the world, the family is extremely important in the formation of his self-concept. The family includes the mothering one, the father, and siblings. The relationship the person has with each of these figures is important, particularly the relationship with the mother. But beyond this, family scholars are teaching us that, as much as any one-to-one

relationship, the place that we are given in the *family system* is important. Every family develops a working order
or system in which each individual plays an assigned role.
These roles help to keep the family functioning. The role
that a child is assigned has as much to do with his self-
estimate as do the relationships he has with individuals
within the family. Some children are required to play roles
in the family that cannot help raising doubts about their
worth.

Quite understandably, the relationship that develops
between the mothering one and the child is important.
Using Erikson's constructs: If the child gains a feeling of
basic trust toward life from the mothering one, he has a
better chance to develop self-esteem than if he gains a
sense of mistrust. Similarly, if the child gains a feeling of
autonomy from the mothering one as she attempts to
socialize the child, he has a better chance to develop self-
esteem than if he obtains a sense of shame. For the most
part, the self-estimate that a child comes to have is not
the result of isolated traumatic events but, rather, the result of "casual conversations, small talk, the easy exchange of ideas, the sharing of minor enthusiasms." [37]

A child often compares himself with his parents. They
are big and they are right—at least they have power. In
comparison, he is small and powerless and, seemingly,
wrong. He needs their help and therefore, in comparison
to them, he appears weak and inadequate. This is the unfortunate picture that a child can easily obtain in his early
years. If he does, he may acquire a low estimate of himself. Likewise the child compares himself unrealistically
and unfairly with older brothers and sisters. When he
competes with them, he does not include the fact that they
are older, but rather, he "knocks" himself when he loses.

Because he lacks more adult powers of reason, the child easily draws negative conclusions about himself. Parental indifference toward a child helps to create feelings of inferiority within the child.[38] For instance, if the parents do not know their child's friends, if they show little or no interest in his progress in school, and if they do not have one meal together as a family, the child gets the feeling that he does not matter much to his parents. This contributes to a low self-estimate. When a child feels that he is being used by his parents, his self-esteem suffers. For instance, when parents believe that their own worth or status is judged by how well their child is doing in comparison with the children of relatives or neighbors, the child is likely to feel used. Or when a child becomes a compensatory device by which parents make up for their own failures, the child may feel used.[39] In either case, the child's self-esteem is in jeopardy. A child may be of psychological value to parents. Allowing a child to develop along with his peers and to gain an increasing amount of independence may pose a threat to parents. To slow this process, parents may keep a child dependent upon them, may deny him free access to other children, or deny him the right to earn money. Parents may belittle a child and undermine his confidence in order to keep the child for their own needs. Parents may feign illness to accomplish the same purpose.[40] Such an approach weakens the child's *maturation process* and puts him at a distinct disadvantage when he compares himself with other children.

Next in importance to his interpersonal relationships with his parents are the child's relationships with his brothers and sisters. By their very presence, other siblings affect the family environment. Birth order may have something to do with the development of inferiority feelings. The oldest child may find parents who feel inadequate to the task of parenting and may pass this insecurity on to the child. The child may feel that he is the one who is not performing properly. A second child may feel that he must compete with the older child. The middle child may not be able to find a niche for himself in the family system and thus feels unwanted or inadequate. The youngest child may feel he has to compete with all his older brothers and sisters for attention. No one position is free from potential inferiority feelings, nor is any position prone toward inferiority feelings. Among the patterns that Rosenberg found are, that an only child has the best chance for high self-esteem, that under certain circumstances, boys have a better chance for high self-esteem, and under other circumstances, girls have a better chance for high self-esteem.[41] The attitude that parents and siblings have toward each child is more important than the birth order. The sex of the child, the timing of his arrival, the economic situation of the family, etc., are among the variables that determine whether or not a child feels wanted, important, and as good as his brothers and sisters. Siblings who sense that they must vie for a place of importance or who feel they must demonstrate their acceptability and worthiness are vulnerable to low self-esteem. When a child senses that, in comparison to his brothers and sisters, he "does not measure up," his self-esteem suffers. If he feels that he is a drag upon the family or that he injures the family image in the community, he will feel poorly about himself.

Life at school can also affect the child's self-estimate. How well or poorly a child does academically is important. Students with good grades tend to have a higher self-estimate than students with low grades.[42] Whether or not a child feels accepted by his peers, particularly by the group of which he would like to be a member, is important in determining whether he feels well or poorly about himself. Traumatic experiences at school, such as being laughed at or reprimanded, may cut very deeply and make a child feel ashamed and inferior.

Holding minority status *in a particular neighborhood* may cause a child to develop feelings of inferiority—even if the child holds majority status *in his nation.* It is the estimate of the child held by the population *in his immediate area* which affects the child. For instance, a white child living in a black community may feel rejected. A Protestant child living in a Jewish community may feel inferior. Even though a child is a member of the majority group *nationally,* if he is a member of a minority group in his neighborhood, he may develop low self-esteem.[43]

A breakup of the family, either through divorce or death, may have a deleterious effect upon a child's self-esteem. Divorce may make a child feel different and therefore inferior. This is particularly acute if there is a stigma attached to divorce in the family's tradition. Adding to the difficulty, before the divorce took place, children are sometimes used by the parents when they battle each other. Finally, a child who needs the emotional support of a stable family, or of one parent, may become anxious and fearful as a result of the family breakup and absence of the needed parent. The death of one parent may have the same effect.

Remarriage, either after divorce or the death of one parent, may also prove difficult for a child. Rosenberg found that if the mother remarried there was a greater chance for the child's self-estimate to be lower than if a mother remained unmarried.[44] In the case of remarriage, instead of a "drawing together" after the initial trauma, the child may feel left out and alone. Having stepparents is associated with low self-esteem. In addition, getting accustomed to a stepparent called for a second readjustment. Rosenberg also found that children who are older at the time of the family breakup are more adversely affected by remarriage than are children who are younger.[45] Apparently the role of the father, which develops later in the child's life, is of real value to the child. The absence of the father has a negative effect upon the child.

Though a low self-estimate is believed to get its start in the early years of childhood, experiences of later childhood and adolescence certainly contribute to low self-esteem as well. Parental disinterest in a youth has the same effect as parental disinterest in a child. William James once wrote:

> No more fiendish punishment could be devised even were such a thing physically possible, than that one should be turned loose in society and remain absolutely unnoticed of all the members thereof.[46]

In a study of high school students, Rosenberg found that parental disinterest contributes to low self-esteem.[47] Indifference on the part of parents causes young people to question whether they mean anything to anyone.[48]

Another cause of low self-esteem in youth is that, instead of either punishing or neglecting a youth, parents disregard the self that the youth is asserting and they attempt to replace it with a self of their own choosing. The youth is liable to feel guilty when he expresses, or wishes to express, his real feelings and he is liable to feel shame at not being himself.[49] Similarly, when a young person feels locked into an identity that he would like to repudiate, but cannot, his self-esteem suffers.[50] This type of parental influence was in the background of a co-ed who acted very spoiled and demanding in her dormitory from the day she entered college. She lost several roommates because she was so selfish. What lay behind this behavior came out when she came for counseling toward the end of her freshman year. She had received word that her mother had attempted suicide. She indicated that her father was an alcoholic and was hard to live with because of his unpredictable behavior. Her mother had tried over the years to "cover" for him since she wished to give the impression that they were a "nice" family and had a "respectable" home. Indeed, the suicide attempt may have been an attempt by the mother to control the father.

Both mother and daughter were living "for" the father. At one point the girl blurted out that she didn't know who she was, what feelings she was supposed to have, or how to behave with others. She didn't want to be that "false" self, but she didn't know how to be anybody else either. She had been accustomed to being deprived of being herself. When she came to college, she indulged herself to make up for her lost years. This only deprived her of friends. Having received prolonged confirmation of a "false" self, she didn't know how to be her "real" self. She was filled with anger and shame. Although the girls with whom she lived had concluded quite the opposite, in counseling it became obvious how poorly she thought of herself.

A low self-estimate may also be caused by parents who give conflicting signals to a youth. When a young person does not receive a consistent definition of himself from his parents—especially when these definitions seem to him mutually exclusive—confusion results, and out of confusion, a low self-estimate. Or, if a youth is made to feel indebted to his parents, he questions his worth. Parents may communicate to a youth that they have done a lot for the youth and that the youth owes them something in return. An adolescent especially is sensitive to his continuing financial dependence, and that point only adds insult to injury with him.

Confused sexual identities in parents can be troublesome for youth. Often this makes youth hesitant in their social relationships. A young man with whom I counseled had a very domineering, possessive, and overprotective mother. She came to the campus on frequent visits. The father was reported to be quiet and passive. The sexual roles in this family were reversed from the normal pattern. As a result, this young man was very insecure. He had little confidence in himself, especially when it came to social relationships. Before coming to college he had won approval by being a "good boy." At college, however, he wished to follow the pattern of his peers, including dating. After gathering all the courage he could, he asked out on a date a young nurse who had tended him while he was in the hospital with a minor ailment. When she politely refused him because she was dating someone else, he was crushed. He lost what little confidence he had in himself, including his established ability as a student. He could not move ahead. He had to drop out of college to seek psychiatric care.

A number of other conditions may also cause a young person to feel inferior. Adolescents who are not dating may feel isolated, rejected, and therefore inferior. A young person who has not found a way to excel or to be recognized may feel worthless. A young person who does not enjoy school but who is too young to obtain a job may feel ashamed, bored, and trapped. His self-esteem may suffer. A young person who is not accepted by a group of his peers among whom he would like to be included may feel rejected and second-rate.

The peculiar status of an adolescent may also contribute to feelings of inferiority. Being neither an adult nor a child, the adolescent may not know what to think of himself nor know how to evaluate himself. Because his status is unclear, his social responsibilities are unclear. He brings the same high level of criticism to bear upon himself that he brings to adult society. He raises doubts about his own abilities and performance. His imagination may conjure up rather grandiose images of himself as an adult, while remnants of his infantile conscience punish him for such dreaming. In short, the adolescent years pose their own hazards for youth just as the early childhood years did for the child.

These are some of the factors that can generate feelings of worthlessness and inferiority in a person. Very often, rather than being caused by one factor, low self-esteem is the result of a combination of factors. And always it is not what the situation *actually* is, but the way the individual reads the evidence that matters.

Inferiority Feelings at Work

The effects of inferiority feelings are both unfortunate and wide-ranging. Rosenberg points out:

What a person thinks of himself . . . is not an imprisoned, encapsulated attitude which has no relevance beyond the borders of his psyche; on the contrary, it extends out into his relationships with other people—guiding, modifying, and controlling them in accordance with its own inexorable logic.[51]

Karen Horney has described how inferiority feelings can structure an individual's life and help to shape his personality as well as his behavior pattern.[52] She contends that, as a result of adverse circumstances in the family, the child sees the world around him as a potentially threatening place. He feels that, *as he is,* he is ill-equipped to cope with it. The child develops basic anxiety. To handle this feeling, he develops a compensatory system. It is this system which becomes the driving force in the individual's life from that point. He looks with contempt upon his "real" self. It is weak and inadequate. In his imagination he develops a better image of himself which Horney calls the "idealized" self. His life takes on neurotic dimensions when he tries to *be* that idealized self. Because it is an idealized self, and quite impossible to realize, he is put into a precarious situation. He needs to keep his real self from being seen by others and must keep up the idealized image as a front. The fact that this whole scheme could come tumbling down causes anxiety in him and makes him try even harder to be the idealized self. Horney calls this the "tyranny of the shoulds." In this person we see perfectionist and compulsive tendencies. He must maintain his idealized image; people must not know about his real self. This need to keep up the idealized image becomes the controlling factor in his life—all this to cover his feelings of inadequacy.

Time and again I see young people fighting a most important battle within themselves. On the one hand, they have feelings that they are basically good, that they have a right to be heard, and that they have a right to feel good about themselves. On the other hand, they hear the voice of their "bad" self reminding them of their inadequacy and inferiority in comparison to others—parents, siblings, cousins, etc. These young people may not be trapped in the kind of neurotic system that Horney describes. Nevertheless, they are in agony. They are engaged in an inner war between their "good" self and their "bad" self.

I counseled, over several years, a young man who was engaged in such a battle. His father and mother were both highly successful professional persons, and his older brother was a straight-A student at one of the leading medical schools in the nation. "And then there is me," he explained. When he first came to college, he was perplexed. At times he felt he should join the military effort, yet he knew that at issue was whether or not he could succeed in college. He remained in college. His second year was filled with frustration. He was very aggressive and frequently was engaged in scuffles, verbal and physical. He finally began to see that he was caught between a need to succeed and a need to fail in order to please the two conflicting feelings he had about himself.

In his third year he found a major and studied very hard. What we found happening in his studies was that he continued to attempt to please both selves. When he took an exam, all the answers he gave were correct; however, he left enough questions unanswered to earn a low grade. When this was pointed out to him, another technique appeared. He answered all the questions on the exam but "inadvertently" he skipped a page, again earning a low grade. By answering all the questions correctly, he pleased his good self, but by leaving a page blank, and therefore earning a low grade, he pleased his bad self. He lived with a very frustrating stalemate, yet he chose the stalemate over allowing either self to gain the upper hand. He could neither move to a better image of himself, nor would he surrender the little self-esteem that he had.

A similar pattern can be seen in some young people who are labeled "underachievers." After testing students who enter the Guided Studies Program, a program designed for underachievers, I found a consistent pattern on the Edwards Personal Preference Schedule. A very high percentage of those tested resisted the self-image of an achiever. In addition, they had a need to be punished, to fail, etc. Though these students have academic ability, their academic performance is affected by their lack of self-esteem.

Low self-esteem affects social relationships. Because an individual has a low estimate of himself, he believes others share this opinion of him. He tends to shy away from others, especially persons he does not know or persons he feels are better than he. His feelings of inferiority limit his social boundaries. Though he would like to join in the fun or conversation that a particular group is having, he fears that they will not want him, that he will be intruding. Choosing to avoid the risk of being rejected, he goes on his way. He is usually oversensitive to criticism. He tends to read things into a conversation that are not necessarily there. In dating, as in other social relationships, he projects his best self, fearing that otherwise he will not be accepted. However, he cannot maintain that self with others forever, and therefore he fears ultimate rejection. Because he feels forced to be dishonest with others, he may develop a cynical attitude toward life. Because he puts up a false front, he feels isolated and alienated from others. His real self never meets other persons, only his false self. For this same reason, he experiences inner fragmentation. This leaves him lonely and confused. Because his real self does not risk exposure or is not allowed exposure, he lives almost as though he were someone else. Yet he is not, and therefore his real self remains rejected and unfulfilled.

To prove his worth to others and to himself, the person with low self-esteem often takes on the image of "worker" or "helper" or both. The worker goes at his work feverishly and with an eye to perfection. The helper feels worthwhile when he has helped someone and when that person responds affirmatively. Since he is never convinced of his worth, the person repeats this pattern endlessly. Indeed, it becomes a need and therefore a personality trait.

Because the person with low self-esteem wishes to be accepted by others, both to prove his worth and to gain interpersonal relationships, he is often guided more by what he thinks will please others than by his own desires, or by what he thinks is right. He is not his own man, but rather a victim of his feelings and needs. Down deep he hates himself because of this lack of integrity. Thus he is caught in a vicious circle.

The person with low self-esteem fears that he is a failure, but to avoid having this established as a final verdict, he may shy away from competition with others or matching himself against a formidable task. While he will not mount evidence that he is worthwhile, neither will he find out for sure what he fears is true. He avoids such a showdown with the truth, or with what he believes to be the truth, by avoiding competition.

A person's low self-esteem may affect his work adversely. After discussing in a marriage counseling session the various ways in which low self-esteem can affect a person, a man discussed the feelings he frequently has while at his job. He is a tool salesman, servicing gasoline stations and garages. He confessed that he often finds himself going right past one of his customers without stopping, thinking to himself—without any objective evidence—that his customer probably doesn't want to see him anyway. He feels that he often takes people's time. He also tries to avoid the pain of hearing people say they don't need anything. When people say this, he takes it personally and feels that it is he whom they are rejecting. To avoid this feeling, he tries to guess whether or not his customers will want to buy something. Obviously his success, or the lack of it, depends more on how he feels about himself than on either the customer's attitudes toward him or the customer's needs.

Finally, because the person with low self-esteem is so preoccupied with his defenses and his needs, he is a very self-centered person. With all of his time and effort spent on himself, he has little time for others, be that in a marriage relationship, in community affairs, or in politics. He tends, therefore, not to be a person who gives but a person who is always attempting to receive.

Conquering Inferiority Feelings

At the beginning of this chapter, I indicated that adolescence is a time of hope. Because he has new mental power and because he is faced with the task of developing his identity, the adolescent has the opportunity and the ability to reevaluate his past. Those adolescents who have low self-esteem and who are plagued with inferiority feelings have an opportunity to draw some new conclusions about themselves. This will not be easy; indeed, it may be very difficult. But it is possible. The following description of how an adolescent may proceed to work toward higher self-esteem comes out of the author's experience with young persons who are engaged in just such a struggle.

A person usually develops low self-esteem as a result of his early life in the family environment. Some of the possible reasons for developing low self-esteem have been listed. The way things appear to him, he is less than he ought to be. He is not living up. He is stupid. He is a liability. He is not meeting expectations, etc. This is the unfortunate conclusion that he develops as he reads the evidence. However, it is very important to understand the following facts:

1. He drew his conclusion on the basis of a *child's mental ability*.
2. His conclusion was based on *his impression* of what other people thought of him, not necessarily on the basis of what they *actually* thought of him.
3. The conclusion that he drew about himself affected his perception in such a way that throughout subsequent life he tended to see only that evidence which supported his thoughts about himself and he failed to see or believe evidence that did not support his feelings.
4. He has lived with that hypothesis ever since, as though it is true.

What the adolescent should understand is that the process whereby he came to a negative conclusion about himself is a faulty one. It is inappropriate for him to live out his life on the basis of a hypothesis that he developed in childhood. He did not have the ability to handle the situation properly. In addition, the authority he gave to parents and siblings is understandable but unfortunate, since parents and siblings also have their problems and may have taken these out on him.

What the adolescent should do is, in his memory, to retrace his steps through his life and recall, insofar as he is able, all the experiences with his peers, in school, and in his family, that either caused or contributed to his feelings of inferiority. I usually work backward from the present environment of the person, through earlier school and family experiences, and finally into early childhood in the home. One purpose of this procedure is to help the young person to see his pattern of life, how he continues to live with an inappropriate hypothesis. It often becomes obvious to the young person that he didn't give himself a chance to refute that hypothesis. The person who is shy and who believes others do not wish to have him participate in their group or informal conversation has never *actually* attempted to break into the group to check whether his feelings are correct or not. For instance, a person may look into the snack bar and see a group of students chatting over coffee. He would like to join them. Instead of actually joining them, he shifts to his imagination. He toys *in his imagination* with joining them. *In his imagination* he finds that they do not wish to have him around. *In his imagination* it turns out to be an abortive attempt, not worth the rejection that he receives. Because it turns out this way *in his imagination,* he does not try it out *in reality.* And yet he uses this evidence *from his imagination* to support the hypothesis. It appears to him that the evidence confirms his feelings, when actually, much, if not all, of that evidence is in his imagination.

A second purpose is to see if the adolescent can determine what cause or causes lie behind his inferiority feelings. It will prove helpful if these can be made conscious, understood, and evaluated in the light of adult reasoning power, as opposed to the limited reasoning power available during childhood. If, for example, his father called him "stupid," the adolescent should search *in the father* for the reasons for this behavior. If siblings appeared more capable, more intelligent, etc., the adolescent should check out *in the total situation* why they appeared so. Perhaps they were older or perhaps the family dynamics were different for them than they were for him. These are the types of reasoning of which a child is incapable. As a result, he lives with an inadequate and distorted picture of himself and his world. What the adolescent must do is bring up as much of the past as he can and evaluate it with adult reasoning power. There is little doubt that he will come up with new and more positive conclusions.

The person with inferiority feelings should also recognize that he drew conclusions about himself on the basis of what *he thought* others thought about him. These conclusions should not go unchecked. Again, traveling back in his memory, the person may be able to come up with a different opinion at important points. Perhaps a conversation with parents or siblings *now* may shed new, and quite a different, light on the subject. As a result he may be able to have higher self-esteem.

This is only one part of the process, and no doubt the easiest part. The more difficult part is breaking out of the old pattern and forming a new one. The old self will put up a life-and-death struggle. Anxiety will become well-nigh intolerable.

What I ask the counselee to do next is attempt to recognize as many places as he can where his feelings of inferiority control his life. In subsequent counseling sessions we discuss how he is affected by this inappropriate hypothesis. It is only as the adolescent recognizes the places where he is affected that he can interrupt his old pattern. For instance, if he would like to be more social or be accepted by his peers when he goes to the snack bar and sees some people sitting at a table, instead of concluding on the basis of his imagination that he will be unwelcome he should gather his courage and join them. Only in this way will he begin to refute what his imagination tells him. It is true that what a person thinks others think of him may be true. It is equally true that, because of his own poor self-image, he has given them an uninteresting picture of himself. This is a vicious circle. That circle needs to be broken at some point. It involves risking rejection. But the chances are that his feelings of inadequacy or worthlessness are more in his own mind than they are in the minds of others.

An individual may improve his self-esteem by setting more realistic goals for himself. If an individual attempts to compensate for his feelings of inferiority or defend himself against his real self, he often establishes unrealistic goals for himself. He attempts to be either perfect or bad. Because he fails to attain his ideal self or reach perfection, he continues to look with disdain upon himself. He is not content to work toward improvement; he usually wishes to arrive at perfection in one grandiose move. What such an individual should do is set smaller, individual goals and work toward the completion of these goals. When he has completed a small task, he should reward himself. By completing a number of small tasks, he may be able to see that he has ability and worth, that it was his techniques that were faulty, not his self. For many persons, the completion of a series of small tasks helps to establish self-confidence and self-esteem. The key is, first, to avoid the "all-or-nothing" system and, second, to recognize and reward oneself for the completion of small tasks.

SUMMARY AND CONCLUSIONS

Because of the stage he is in, the adolescent has an opportunity to raise his self-estimate. Feelings of inferiority usually develop in early childhood, although later experiences may also contribute. The quality of his interpersonal relationships within the family, particularly with the mothering one, are especially important. Inferiority feelings affect persons in a variety of ways. The person may develop compensatory drives to cover his real feelings and to prove his worthwhileness. He may experience an inner war between a "good" self and a "bad" self. Inferiority feelings can cause social relationships to be awkward and quite unrewarding. His work may also be hurt as a result of a lack of self-confidence. He may be self-centered, concerned more about his own well-being and less about the well-being of others. Though it is not easily accomplished, self-esteem can be improved. Seeing that he drew his conclusions as a child and that these may be inaccurate and inappropriate in the light of adult reason, the person may be able to develop a more positive self-image. Finding the reasons why he developed this negative self-image, locating the many ways in which these feelings affect his life, and realizing that it was a subjective conclusion not necessarily based on reality, the person may be able to break out of his old image and behavior patterns.

The human being seems to have an innate urge to have a positive attitude toward himself. The Judeo-Christian tradition has held that every man should have a positive estimate of himself. The humanist position is that all men have a right to self-esteem. Each person should live with a positive hypothesis about his worth. It is unfortunate when a person has low self-esteem. This is the assumption of this book. It is hoped that readers who suffer from feelings of inferiority will be able to exorcise the negative feelings they have and come to a new and happier view of themselves.

7

THE TASKS OF LATE ADOLESCENCE
AND EARLY ADULTHOOD

There is no clear boundary between the work a youth does in early and middle adolescence and the work he faces in late adolescence and early adulthood. Establishing an identity is an ongoing process. Nevertheless, there is a different emphasis in the later years. In Chapter 2, we saw the young adolescent attempting to break away from his parents, handling his infantile conscience, becoming acquainted with his new body, including his sexual drives, and attempting to gain his independence. The emphasis was upon loosening earlier identifications and patterns and handling the new emotional climate that this produced. In contrast to this emphasis, the work of late adolescence and early adulthood is putting together an identity and integrating its many parts into a working whole.

The Growing Sense of Responsibility

If early and middle adolescence is marked by a movement *away* from parents, late adolescence is characterized by a movement *toward* independence and an autonomous existence. Indeed, any youth who has reached this stage but who senses lingering dependence upon his parents is liable to experience feelings of inadequacy if not panic. In late adolescence there is even less contact with parents than before. With greater freedom from his parents, the young person often indulges in a variety of ideas, estimates of reality, and identities. He may feel misled by the black-and-white categories into which his parents placed life and may indulge even more deeply in "foreign" ideas, or he may explore various points of view just for the mere excitement of it.

There is a sense of play that carries over from earlier years. Experiences are intense, emotional, and real to a youth; and yet, most of the time he is aware that life is not yet hard reality. On the other hand, the line of demarcation between playing at being an adult and *being* an adult is increasingly difficult to distinguish, both for the adolescent and for an observer. A young person knows that a higher level of responsibility is expected of him and he has the desire to be an adult. Yet there is a fear of having to establish his identity and take on the responsibility of adulthood.

An important shift takes place in the structure of morality in the person in late adolescence and young adulthood. Earlier in life it was up to others to establish and enforce morality. A youth responded affirmatively or negatively to the rules that his parents, school officials, and other adults established. He was not supposed to question the morality expected of him. His pattern of ethical behavior was to respond to externally imposed standards. But with late adolescence and early adulthood comes a radical shift. As he gains his independence, he realizes that he is not responsible to others so much as he is responsible to himself and for himself. His life is now in his own hands! Only *he* can make it significant and meaningful. The adolescent ponders such questions as Who am I? and What shall I become? And though this entails a certain amount of introspection, in the long run this is the route by which a young person begins to take a new stance in life, one of responsibility for himself and for the world in which he lives. Instead of asking, What can I get by with? he asks, What kind of life do I want? and What kind of world do I wish to live in?

In addition to a new basis for morality, a person in late adolescence and early adulthood gains a new perspective on time—past, present, and future. Earlier, time was only an abstract notion. A child's experience with time was only in learning how to tell time, in seeing to it that he went to school and came home on time, and in devoting given amounts of time to certain activities, such as music lessons. In late adolescence and early adulthood all that changes. Time takes on new meaning. This is the result of the new mental equipment which a youth acquires in adolescence.

Though a youth had always had some notion of the future, now the future takes on new dimensions. Thomas Oden writes:

> To gaze upon the future is to gaze upon an abyss of possibilities, totally void of any actualized meaning. Nothing has ever happened in the future. For the future is precisely that expected range of time in which nothing has yet happened. It is just open—filled with the nothingness of possibility.[53]

It begins to dawn upon the adolescent that each person exists in relation to the future in a deeply personal way. The future looms before him as a possibility and as a threat. The future holds his destiny. It is where he will find fulfillment, affirmation, and meaning, or where he will fail, where all of his fears about his inadequacy will come true. It is where his possibilities lie and, at the same time, where he may be unmasked. There is an innate desire in a young person to move ahead and affirm his worth and meaning, to actualize his possibilities, and yet there is some fear of the future. He can no longer lean upon others. He faces the future by himself.

One reason why the future is a threat to an adolescent is that his identity is not firmly formed. He does not feel ready to be evaluated or judged in his present state. He wishes to bring his best possibilities with him into the future, but he is not sure which these are. Therefore, he would like to forestall foreclosure. On the other hand, *not* to move ahead is itself failure. This is the challenge and the predicament of late adolescence and early adulthood.

In late adolescence and early adulthood, the person discovers the connection between time, values, and identity. Time is an extension of a person. How he uses his time says something about himself. What he does says something about who he is. And what he does in the present has consequences for the future. If before, a youth could respond rather freely to the pleasure principle, now he can no longer do so without that response becoming a part of his value system and therefore his identity. This realization creates a new seriousness and a new sense of responsibility within a person.

The *passing* of time is another dimension of time that a young person grasps. In Rudolph Wittenberg's words, a youth realizes that "time is running out, that role playing will have to be terminated shortly, that long-range and binding choices and decisions will have to be made." [54] Indeed, the adolescent begins to sense how valuable time actually is! He senses that he has an indeterminate amount of time during which society expects him to perform certain responsibilities. But more important than this, a youth senses that he has only a limited amount of time with which to work. In this time he must establish who he is and hope that *as that identity,* he will prove of value to himself and to others. Though the pressure may at first appear to be external, i.e., society's expectations of him, there is a growing realization within a youth that it is to himself that he must prove his worth, his meaning.

A person's imagination plays a crucial role in identity formation. Only in his imagination can a person venture into the future. In his imagination the adolescent can try out ideas, opinions, estimates of reality, identities, etc. He searches for that combination which, as close as he can guess, will bring affirmation and fulfillment. Through the use of his imagination the adolescent attempts to second-guess what identity will work for him.

Repudiation and Commitment

In early and middle adolescence, a person gains a smorgasbord of opinions, behavior patterns, estimates of reality, and identifications. From these he must ultimately form his own identity. As long as he feels safely within the moratorium, a youth will wish to keep open as many options as possible. To make final selections at this early stage appears to the youth as submission, i.e., loss of individuality, acceptance of responsibility, and accountability to others.[55] Such a move appears to a youth to make his world smaller just at a time when he wishes to make it larger. There is a tendency to resist any kind of decision that would narrow the youth's choices. On the other hand, a youth knows that he cannot form his identity while keeping all these options open. When a youth senses that his time is running out, he begins to narrow his choices. Narrowing his choices and forming his identity is a two-fold movement, like two sides of a coin. First, it involves repudiation, discarding those elements which will not be used in his identity. Second, it involves committing himself to those elements which will be incorporated in his identity.

Repudiation is an important means of alleviating identity diffusion. It implies at least a tentative ordering of values and some feeling for an identity. However, precisely because one's identity is still open and because repudiation may involve discarding values, opinions, and estimates of reality held by important others, it may be an agonizing process. Repudiation may prove particularly difficult if it entails going against the values and hopes that parents held out for the youth, especially when it is the nature of that youth to want to please his parents. The values, patterns, and identities of older siblings may also be difficult for a youth to handle.

The parents of a girl with whom I worked were both well educated and engaged in educational occupations. Education was a high value in their home. Two older siblings went through college with honors and on to graduate school. But their third daughter seemed to have less academic ability. She also seemed to have different personality needs. These were not being met in the academic community. Yet she could not break out and "do her thing." On the one hand, there were her family's values and older siblings living by these values. On the other hand, she had her own notions about herself—her abilities, her needs, her feelings, her imagination of what would be meaningful for her. Since her own identity was still open, she could not be sure of her own feelings. These did not have enough "authority" to allow her to break with her past pattern of pleasing her parents. Repudiation of this particular value, i.e., higher education, proved difficult.

Breaking with the values and patterns of peers may prove just as difficult as breaking with parental values and patterns. Wittenberg posed one of youth's dilemmas:

Does he align himself with right-thinking people although he does not like the way they behave—or with the very friendly people whose opinions he does not accept? [56]

The division between parents and peers is a tough one to handle. The adolescent may feel like a stranger to himself as he attempts to respond to pressures from all sides. He must repudiate if he is to move ahead toward the formation of his identity.

Having repudiated those opinions, values, and identities which, according to his growing sense of self, he cannot use, a young person begins to sort out those few values, opinions, etc., which seem important and integral to his growing sense of identity. He begins to commit himself to these. In doing so, his self-picture takes further shape and strength. He knows more clearly who he is. Diffusion begins to disappear and a life-style or a sense of self is established. Once this stage has been reached, it is much easier for the person to make decisions. He now has a point of reference to evaluate the forces that he encounters. More and more he is able to commit himself to people and causes because he can tell whether these coincide and support his sense of self or not. He is much more familiar with himself. Having reached this stage of comfort with himself, he is no longer so concerned with himself, but can begin to reach out with less fear toward others. In Erik Erikson's framework, when a youth has reached this stage of identity formation, he moves on to the next task of intimacy.

The Role of an Ideology in Identity Formation

Having gained his independence from his parents, and wishing to be an autonomous individual, a youth can no longer live by the philosophy of life or ideology of his parents. Nor does he want to. On the other hand, neither does a new ideology simply arise from the opinions, values, and identifications from which he is shaping his unique identity. Acquiring an ideology is a separate and specific task that each youth faces. Gordon Allport describes an ideology as "a clear comprehension of life's purpose in terms of an intelligible theory" and as "a unifying philosophy of life." [57] An ideology may be thought of more narrowly as the cause, within a larger understanding of life, to which a youth gives himself. However it is conceived, it contains an orderly and meaningful overall scheme of things and a compelling vision with which a youth can identify. The process of forming an identity is greatly enhanced by the acquisition of an ideology.

An ideology is often very demanding. It calls for a high level of commitment and rigid discipline as well, abilities that a youth, it is hoped, has acquired. It may call for total obedience to a theory or tradition, total resignation, total inner reform, total abandon, or total commitment to a cause. But young people who have reached this stage are often willing to make such a commitment. Usually no price is too high to pay in the interest of the ideology. The Red Guard in China is an illustration.

If an ideology is pursued at a high cost, a youth receives many benefits. An ideology helps young people move into the future. Most of the ideologies to which young people give themselves are idealistic and promise new hope for society. The cause is always understood as superior to past ideologies. The ideology is heralded as that force which will right past wrongs, rejuvenate society, bring back glory to the nation, etc. Continuity with forgotten ideals is emphasized. Such an ideology gives young people a meaningful picture of the future and therefore helps them move ahead.

Without the possibility of choosing a new course of action, young people feel trapped. They feel as if their lives are determined and as if they don't make any difference. Young people need to feel that they count for something. They cannot live off someone else's identity or integrity. They must feel that they can reverse the course of history, or at least change its direction and thus leave their mark upon it. They must feel as if history has room for them. Young people, as individuals and collectively as a generation, must feel that they can "do their own thing."

By associating himself with what appears to be the way of the future, a youth feels that his life, in contrast to the lives of members of the older generation, will be relevant. This is especially acute in a rapidly changing society such as ours, when the values, patterns, and identities of the older generation appear to the youth to be irrelevant. Young people gain a feeling of confidence when they feel they will improve on the past. Often there is less discontinuity with the past than either the older or the younger generation thinks. Usually young people take the forgotten ideals of the past and attempt to succeed where they believe their parents failed. Such programs as the Peace

Corps and VISTA, as well as programs sponsored by religious groups, offer young people the opportunity to do something significant for society. These are new programs and thus capture the imagination of youth, and yet they are based upon the ideals and principles held by previous generations.

An ideology gives a youth a central purpose which draws his identity together into an integrated whole. An ideology acts like glue in holding his identity together firmly. The boundaries of his personality become more clearly established. It is easier for him to decide on the values he will pursue. Repudiation is made easier, as is commitment.

In giving himself to a particular ideology, a young person finds a cause by which to measure himself. In the past he was unable to commit himself for any period of time because his identity was still in flux. Now he gives himself totally and unconditionally and thereby finds out the extent of his abilities and power. He pits himself against others to find out the boundaries of his self as well as to find out how his abilities compare with the abilities of others. In addition, by giving himself totally to the cause, he becomes a part of that cause and gains whatever prestige it gives him.

Finding an ideology may prove helpful to a youth in other ways as well. The group identity and companionship may fill a void left when he broke away from home. He is cheered by the companionship of his peers, who share the same ideology. In addition, giving his thoughts and energies to a cause beyond himself, the young person focuses less on his inadequacies and fears. Further, energy that might otherwise be channeled into aggressive drives and sexual impulses is handled more comfortably and constructively in the form of work directed toward the cause. Adult society responds more favorably toward such behavior, and the young person himself realizes its value.

An ideology may be politically oriented, as in the case of the young people who worked for Senator Eugene McCarthy. It may be racially oriented, as in the case of the Hitler Youth Movement. It may be socially oriented, as in the case of the civil rights movement. And obviously, it may entail a combination of these. In addition, religion may serve as an ideology, although not everyone who is religious is guided by a religious ideology. Gordon Allport points out that the faith of some people is such that it provides them with "an inclusive solution to life's puzzles in the light of an intelligible theory." [58] Their faith becomes the integrative and motivational factor of their lives. For other people religion merely serves their self-interest. For them religious beliefs and activities are simply holdovers from childhood that are used to support the immediate interests and needs of the individual.

A religion has potential as an ideology. Allport writes:

> That which is ever not quite fulfilled is best able to hold the attention, guide effort, and maintain unity. It is for this reason that religion qualifies as an integrative agent *par excellence*. Precisely because religious accomplishment is always incomplete, its cementing character in personal life is therefore all the greater. [59]

However, if a person's religion is to serve as his ideology, it will have to be updated as he goes through the developmental stages from childhood to adulthood. In childhood, religious rituals were learned but their significance was not understood. If a person is going to have a mature faith, one that can serve as an ideology, he will have to understand the significance of such rituals. Frequently an adolescent and young adult will abandon the rituals he was taught in childhood. Part of the reason is that he does not understand them and therefore they have little meaning for him. Perhaps the greater reason has to do with changes that take place in his mental abilities and needs at this stage. Theological, ethical, moral, and philosophical concerns hold his attention. He asks deep and searching questions. Ritual interests him less, especially if he does not understand it. If the faith with which he was raised is to be a live option as his ideology, it will have to help him pursue the questions with which he is wrestling at this stage.

If a person's faith is to be a live option as an ideology, it will have to allow modification in understanding from the literal way he understood things in childhood to a more abstract and universal interpretation that fits his nature in late adolescence and early adulthood. If a religious tradition resists such adaptation, it forces a person to maintain a childhood level of interpretation in adulthood or forces him to reject his faith. On the other hand, if faith can be adapted, this can be a time of great excitement when a young person is able to change to a more abstract and universal interpretation of his faith.

Finally, if religion is to serve as an ideology for a young person, it must be open to new language, new doctrinal formulations, new ethical guidelines, new rituals, etc. Faith must express the mood of contemporary youth and seem relevant to the issues of the day. For example, whereas the sovereignty and majesty of God were important concepts for earlier generations, the immanence of God is important to contemporary young people. Whereas correct doctrinal formulations were important to earlier generations, ethical concerns captivate youth. They wish to broaden and deepen the command to "love your neighbor." As a part of this shift in emphasis, hymns that use military metaphors, such as "Onward Christian Soldiers," or that refer to God as Victor and King, are avoided. Youth have abandoned the pipe organ with its majesty and complexity and have turned to folk music accompanied by the guitar for its simplicity and ethical emphasis. Liturgical worship, with its forced community, has been exchanged for the spontaneity and community of small and informal group activities. And youth are interested in a faith that has contemporary application as opposed to promises about the afterlife.

When a young person turns to his religious tradition for his ideology, he needs to peel off much of the wrapping that had gathered earlier. He needs to locate the bedrock concepts of that faith. He will bring these to bear upon the present. If this is possible, then faith can become an ideology. When faith is adaptable to the needs of youth, it can continue to serve them. That religion which understands the needs and nature of youth will have the best chance of serving as an ideology for them.

Intimacy and Commitment

Having formed his self-image this securely, a young person gains the ability to relate to other people in concrete affiliations and partnerships, particularly with the opposite sex. He has less fear that he will be confused by others or swallowed up by stronger identities. Earlier, without knowing precisely who he was, the young person related to others with some fear. Because he was fearful, his associations might be quite aggressive or exploitive if for no other reason than out of defense. Now, however, with less fear he can relate with much more confidence. Because he is not as threatened, he is capable of deeper relationships. Instead of being aggressive and exploitive, he is able to be more considerate, even tender, in his relationships. Because he no longer needs to direct all his energy toward himself, he gains a greater ability to care for others. The quality of his interpersonal relationships is greatly enhanced.

One of the last places where a young person gains confidence is in his sexual identity. First through casual and group relationships and later through more serious and intimate relationships, a young person becomes comfortable with his sexual identity. Gradually through experience, he is able to relate as a male or female to someone of the opposite sex at increasingly intimate depths. As a result, his interest in sharing life with someone of the opposite sex grows in intensity.

Sometime during late adolescence or early adulthood, most young people gain the ability to commit themselves to a person of the opposite sex in a marital bond. Earlier the intensity and permanence of such a relationship would have been threatening. Now, however, with a well-formed identity and with an orientation *toward* others, a person is able, indeed wants, to commit himself to another person.

Young people gain the ability for intimacy and the ability to make and keep commitments at different ages. They may have many of the characteristics of adulthood and yet may not have these two important abilities. There is an indeterminate gap between the development of the sex drive and the ability to be intimate, just as there is a gap between the ability to be intimate and to make and keep commitments. Physical maturation precedes emotional maturation.

A sophomore co-ed who had been an excellent student was referred to the counseling center because she suddenly lost interest in her studies. She could not explain her plight when she came in, but it soon became apparent that she felt trapped in a life-style and was attempting to break free from it. She was known by her parents, members of the church she attended, and her community as a well-behaved, talented, and intelligent person. However, while in college her interests and values began changing. She had not dated, but wanted to date. The occupation she had in mind seemed more like one imposed upon her rather than one of her own choosing. She confessed that she would really like to be a different person than the person people knew her as—not too different, but just enough to feel that she had chosen her identity.

In a series of counseling sessions we attempted to explore options. We imagined occupations that would use her talents and would allow her to be married. These occupations also had to fit her emerging ideology. We also worked on updating her faith. After several sessions of counseling she was released to see if she could develop an identity out of these possibilities.

Several months later she came in to discuss a problem. She had dated a particular young man since shortly after counseling began. This young man was soon to be graduated from college. He had his occupational future all planned. He was at the stage when marriage would put the finishing touches on his identity. She was complimented and pleased by this turn of events, but was also uneasy. She wondered whether this was the normal pattern that was followed. Was she "on course" or not?

I felt it was important to tell her that, though she was nineteen and therefore had reached an age when some people get married, her situation warranted some concern. Just three months earlier she had never dated. Indeed, her identity was completely unsettled. Her occupational plans were very uncertain. I indicated that it is hazardous to enter marriage when these psychological tasks are unfinished. Marriage under these conditions is a risk. What she needed was more time to find and solidify her self. If she married before these tasks were completed, she risked having to handle a great number of changes in her personality in early marriage.

Young people at this age have reached marriageable age. They have strong sex drives. Yet they may not have completed the psychological work necessary to have a strong self-image and a stable marriage.

When a young person gains the ability to be intimate and to make and keep commitments, he is ready to find a marriage partner. The choice of a marriage partner is closely tied to his self-picture. He cannot choose a person who will overwhelm his identity nor one who would not share many of his values. A marriage partner must be chosen who complements his own self-image. In this sense, he should not choose a partner before his identity is formed. At the same time, finding a suitable partner helps to solidify the self.

If a person does not gain this ability to be intimate, he lives with a feeling of isolation. Such a person has highly structured and stereotyped relationships with others. He goes through the motions of intimacy but does not experience a real meeting of persons. Such a person may experience bewilderment and self-doubt and have an overall feeling of isolation from others.

A young man who had not gained the ability to be intimate came for counseling. He was older than most students, although he did not give that appearance. On campus he was extremely outgoing, known by everyone. He could keep children amused by his antics and older people enthralled in conversation. But he confessed tearfully that he felt isolated from people his own age. He had had several rapid courtships in the past in which there was talk of marriage. But each time he reached a certain point, he became afraid and the relationship deteriorated. The relationship in which he was currently involved was following that same pattern. He expressed his fears over his masculinity. He often went to work or found something else to do instead of taking out his girl. The high ethical standard he held for himself was a defense. His girl was becoming increasingly dissatisfied with their relationship because she was ready for increasing levels of intimacy.

The virtues that Erikson sees rising out of identity formation and intimacy are fidelity and love. A youth who has attained this level of maturity can remain committed to his partner in spite of contradictions in values and other adverse conditions that may periodically prevail. Though he has needs that must be met, he can give a great deal of his time and attention to caring for others.

A young college couple came for marriage counseling. They were near the point of getting a divorce. They had been married about two years. The husband was graduating from college in a few months and planned further study toward a profession. His wife was working to support the couple. They were young when they married. They had felt then that they were in love. As they reflected upon it now, their sexual urges as well as other needs probably had led them to marriage. The wife was still in love, but

the husband was not. He was busy with his studies, but
even more busy with political involvement. Indeed, he
spent hours in political activities. He was trying to make
this country a more just place in which to live. An ideology now captured his vision and energy. To him, this was
more important than a marriage that obviously was not
working. In private he confessed that he could not maintain the kind of intimacy that marriage entailed. He was
still struggling with broad philosophical questions as well
as with occupational questions. Graduate school was as
much *obtaining more time* as it was preparing for an occupation.

Though this young man had thought he was in love and
on that basis had entered marriage, he had not yet gained
the ability for sustained intimacy, nor of making and
keeping commitments, and, therefore, he had not gained
the virtues of fidelity and love. It was ironic how he could
talk about helping humanity at the same time that he was
abandoning his marriage.

The Role of Occupational Choice in Identity Formation

If finding an ideology is important in forming and solidifying an identity, so is making an occupational choice.
Indeed, the inability to settle on an occupation leads to
continued identity diffusion.

Choosing an occupation is not an activity restricted to
late adolescence and early adulthood. It is an ongoing
process that begins in childhood and culminates in the late
teens and early twenties. Nevertheless, as Eli Ginzberg
points out, there are recognizable stages in the process.
First, there are the choices made in fantasy by a child as

he dreams of adulthood. Later, tentative occupational choices are made by a child at approximately age eleven. These are made on the basis of *early estimates* of interests, abilities, and values. Finally, beginning at approximately age seventeen, the young person pursues occupational choices more realistically and intently. During this stage, there is exploration first. This is followed by the crystallization of a broad occupational area. Finally focus is made upon one specific occupation.[60]

A person should not conclude from this that these are neat categories which do not overlap. Indeed, the imagination can be used very beneficially in the late teens and early twenties during the exploratory stage. Nor should a person conclude, as I have seen many college students do, that once a college major is chosen, or once an occupation is entered, a person's occupational future is set. There is room for change in later years, though an occupation that calls for a different educational background or that would require a totally different type of personality is quite unlikely.

As a young person works at choosing his occupation, he may be realistic in his explorations and in his tentative choices, or he may be quite unrealistic, depending upon his ego-strength. The stronger a person's ego, the more conscious he is of his needs. He will be able to balance all the factors that go into his decision and therefore be realistic in his occupational choice. The more unstable and weak a person's ego, the more chance there is that his imagination will wander in unrealistic directions. The person who has self-confidence can see his strengths and weaknesses, whereas the person who lacks self-confidence is less able to handle his strengths and weaknesses. He may look upon his occupation as a means of bolstering his self-esteem. His imagination may be unreliable for occupational planning.

The process of choosing an occupation is integrally related to the process of identity formation. Indeed, an individual's occupation is a part of his identity. A person's early environment, including the personalities of his parents, the cultural climate of his home, the role he played in the family, the values of his family, etc., shape both his occupational choice and his identity. In addition, his mental ability, physical traits, energy, etc., as well as the social environment in which he hopes to live, affect both his vocational choice of occupation and his identity. The self and the occupation are integrally related. A person's occupation is an extension of himself. It, therefore, must fit his identity. The process of occupational development is essentially that of developing and implementing a self-concept.

There is disagreement over whether the identity is formed before a firm occupational choice is made or whether making the choice helps to solidify the identity. It may be that the process differs with individuals. Whichever it is, there is no doubt that choosing an occupation is closely related to solidifying the identity of a youth. Likewise, the inability to find an occupation leads to continued identity diffusion.

There are other benefits for a youth who has made his occupational choice. For the first time in his life, he will be paying his own way, or, if he is still in training, he may at least anticipate paying his own way. He gains a feeling of autonomy and worth. Since an occupation is an extension of the self, when he enters his occupation, he establishes his social and economic status in society and further solidifies his identity. In his occupation, he is also able to demonstrate his abilities. This aids his self-esteem. Finally he has reached the point of being a productive member of society. This gives him the mark of adulthood, something which he has sought, and which says to him that his identity is accepted.

SUMMARY

In late adolescence and early adulthood a person develops a greater sense of responsibility. Instead of responding to external stimuli, he begins to see that he is responsible for himself. Handling the future is seen as the key to whether or not he will have meaning. In order to curb identity diffusion, a youth must repudiate those elements which will not help in forming his identity and learn to commit himself to those values which hold promise for him. As he moves ahead in the process of repudiation and commitment, his identity becomes more firm. An ideology also helps in the process of identity formation. An ideology gives a youth a framework to understand life and offers him a way to find meaning for his life. It gives him a central core of values and thereby pulls his identity firmly together. It also gives him a bridge to the future. When the individual's self is established, he dares to relate to other people more intimately, especially persons of the opposite sex. The more solid his self-image, the more free the individual is to care for others. Since an occupation is an extension of an individual, it is closely associated with the process of identity formation. In addition to helping to solidify his self-image, selecting an occupation brings recognition of the individual's identity by society as well as his acceptance into adulthood by that society.

8

THE MOODS, FEELINGS, AND DEFENSES OF LATE ADOLESCENCE AND EARLY ADULTHOOD

During early adolescence it may have appeared to a youth that everything had come loose. This was his concern. In late adolescence a youth may wonder whether he will ever be put together in a workable and acceptable way. This is his concern. The tasks that he faces during this stage are important and difficult ones. He is also very aware that his time is running out. This predicament leads to a variety of moods, feelings, and defenses that are somewhat peculiar to this stage.

Many contemporary adolescents and young adults handle the tasks and problems that they face during this stage through a close identification with contemporary youth culture. They find solace in the group. This movement, with its clothing and hairstyles, and distinctive music, serves to "legitimize" their moods, feelings, and actions. We will first look at the moods and feelings of contemporary young people by focusing on contemporary youth culture.

Contemporary Youth Culture

Some centuries ago, men dreamed of finding a better life for a greater number of people. They toppled feudal society with a combination of two new approaches to life. First, they used money as a means of making money. Second, they accepted the new scientific theories and techniques. Both the new business ethos and the new scientific theories paid off. The growing middle class assured itself of a better life by wedding business and science to form a technological society. America was discovered as a result of this technology. She gathered to her shores millions of immigrants who were looking for a better life for themselves and their children. Finding a better life via technology, Americans adopted the values and style of life to assure the continuation of that technological society.

However, this style of life, with its underlying values, is considered by many contemporary youths to be *against* man. And young people are attempting to establish an alternate set of attitudes, values, and style of life. If they were to accept the values and life-style of the technological society, many young people would feel that they "were 'selling out,' abandoning their dreams and visions, committing themselves to people, institutions, and causes which they see as making destructive claims on them." [61]

In turning against the values of the older generation, what young people dislike the most is the fragmentation of life that results from a technology-oriented life-style. The individual and the society as a whole experience fragmentation. Technology may bring a higher standard of living, but it is at the cost of wholeness within the self as well as wholeness within the family of man.

Contemporary youth are looking for an alternative to the nuclear family. Made up of parents and a few siblings, and living at a distance from relatives, the nuclear family is much more intense and isolated than was the extended family. The extended family included parents, a larger number of siblings, and often a grandparent or two and possibly an uncle or aunt. In addition, the extended family lived in the vicinity of a host of relatives. Because it is so intense, the nuclear family mediates to youth the pressures and frustrations that parents, living by technology-oriented values, feel. Youth feel the pressure of upward mobility. They pick up the competitiveness between husband and wife as well as between siblings. Because of its small size, the nuclear family offers only a limited number of relationships and identities. Its youthful members often sense lack of meaning in their parents' lives. Youth feel that the nuclear family is narrow and selfish and lacks the larger perspective and concern that they feel man should have. Thus, the nuclear family is contributing to the process of fragmentation in society.

The occupations available in a technological society promote inner fragmentation and lead to a loss of meaning in the individual. Paul Goodman points out that though there is nearly full employment, there are fewer jobs that are *necessary and unquestionably useful,* jobs that draw upon man's abilities and energy and which, therefore, contribute to his dignity.[62] Instead of producing meaning in a person's life, many jobs produce only money. With only money and the things that it can buy as his reward, man becomes interested only in making a "fast buck." Making money enhances one's standard of living, but it is a living that is not interesting or meaningful. Goodman has this penetrating observation: "When one does nothing, one is threatened by the question, *is* one nothing?" [63]

Specialization, another feature of our technological society, also leads to fragmentation. Specialization disregards man's essential wholeness. It demands that one part of him be very highly trained whereas other abilities, interests, or dimensions be repressed. In addition, specialization asks man to give himself exclusively to a very small but intense job that is only one part of the whole task. As a result, he does not feel related to the finished product. He feels that his life is in the service of technology. Still further, in earlier societies, a man's occupation often supplied him with an integrative element in his life. His occupation helped to define who he was. Specialization robs him of this. Contemporary specialized man is hard pressed to find an integrative element for his life.

Technology has fragmented man because it places a premium upon the cognitive abilities of man and gives a subordinate position to feelings. The uniquely human concept of feelings has had to take a backseat to such concepts as efficiency, productivity, and practicality. A significant dimension of man has had to be repressed. Again, at this point, man has been made to feel that his wholeness must be sacrificed for technology—a price that contemporary young people are saying is too high a price to pay.

Life in our technology-oriented society is conceived as being filled with problems. Our technology gives us the *techniques* by which we solve life's problems. This understanding has given us a peculiar approach to life. Kenneth Keniston describes both the process and the results:

> We normally assume that the pitfalls along life's path can best be dealt with by treating them as cognitive difficulties whose solution involves the application of

"know-how." Ours is a how-to-do-it society and not a what-to-do society. For every discussion of the ethics of love, we have a dozen manuals in every drug store on the "techniques" of love. For every discussion of the purpose of life, industry, and society, a thousand hours are spent in discovering how to sell soap, how to peddle the image of a politician, how to propagate the "American way of life." We approach even the question of national survival as a cognitive problem of how to ready ourselves to destroy the Russians efficiently should the need arise, and how to limit their effective capacity to destroy us. Our human troubles and tragedies are largely defined as "unsolved problems"; and our chief attention goes toward attempting to discover the proper cognitive techniques for solving them. Thus our society characteristically dismisses "final questions" as either philosophically "meaningless" or—more commonly—as "irrelevant" to the pressing problems at hand. The man who insists on asking such questions is usually considered an obstructionist. Discussions of "why" and "what" are relegated to Sunday church-going, to neurotic adolescents, and to a few artists and dissidents whose views are occasionally reported, well behind the business news, in our national weeklies.[64]

Under the influence of technology and its accompanying values, we disregard one extremely important dimension of man—the ethical dimension.

Our society has tended to produce technicians rather than philosophers. If the discussion over the war in Indochina has pointed out little else, it has drawn attention to two contrasting approaches to life—the technical and the ethical. This fragmentation explains—though it in no way justifies—the easy acceptance in America of the terrible weapons of war that have been produced by technology. Technology has led to the loss of a critical approach to life from an ethical point of view. It has led to the loss of an ethical consciousness in American society.

Technology has led to a greater understanding of nature than man has ever had before and, at the same time, has led to alienation from nature. Throughout history, man has attempted to understand and control nature. But not until this era has man gained such a degree of understanding and control. He has gone beyond the point of understanding nature to the point of exploiting it. His approach to nature has grown methodical and analytic. He has lost touch with nature. Man has learned to look at nature through one stereotyped approach, that of the scientific method. He relates to nature via the fragments that he puts under the close scrutiny of the microscope. No longer does man simply enjoy nature in its totality.

Young people are against the American business ethos which pits man against man in a competitive and often combative way. Raised in a competitive society, in families that competed with their neighbors, by parents who used their children for purposes of prestige and upward mobility, society which talks of peace but which is engaged in war after war, young people have had enough of competitiveness and combativeness. They are ignoring the lines along which competition and combativeness have been drawn and which have fragmented their existence.

Many young people have found it difficult to form an identity in our technological and rapidly changing society. A reason for this is that technological man lacks an integrative element in his life. Keniston captures the dilemma:

> When asked the terrifying question, "Who are you?"
> we can reply with a list of our social memberships,
> our roles, and even our personal characteristics.
> "Businessman, father of three, Rotarian, Methodist,
> Republican, homeowner, and decent man"—the list
> often contains only the unity of outer correlation,
> and leaves the speaker with a vague sense of being
> harried and harassed, of having no vital center, of
> being only what he does and of doing things that
> have no relationship to each other or to the central
> self.[65]

Young people have seen this in their parents and are looking for something else.

Another factor making it difficult for young people to form an identity in our technological and rapidly changing society has to do with the changing concept of time which has arisen among youth growing up in that society. Young people have been more sensitive than adults about the weapons of war that have been devised. Add the existence of these incomprehensibly destructive weapons together with the fact that America has been in repeated wars during the twentieth century, and young people do not get a very enticing picture of the future. They would rather disassociate themselves from adulthood and remain, at least for a while longer, in the relatively more carefree state of adolescence.

Further, technological innovations have come so rapidly that commitment to a specific future, and therefore *to the future,* is difficult for youth. The images that their parents followed are inadequate for youth. The past seems totally irrelevant to them, and young people are seeing present images, occupations, and values become outdated. There-fore, young people are left without viable images to fol-low. If they reject the images that adults presently hold, it is easy for them to reject *adulthood* in the process, es-pecially when youth cannot get an impression of what might serve them in the future.

With our technology, changes occur so rapidly that people begin to feel that, rather than controlling history, *man is controlled by history.* This has serious implications for youth. There is a tendency to lose a feeling of im-portance and dignity if man is merely an object, or worse, the victim of history. What does it mean to be responsible under such conditions? As a result there is a tendency by youth, if not by adults, to live for the present, rather than build for the future. This may explain why there has been a growing emphasis upon immediate gratification of needs and an interest in the senses. If the future is no longer a compelling entity, how does a person develop an identity? In the past, an identity had been formed as a person matched himself against the future.

Finally, without a tie to the past, because it is irrelevant, and without an eye to the future, because it is too doubt-ful, man loses his sense of orientation. He feels lost. He doesn't know where he came from, nor where he is going. To form an identity, both past and future play crucial roles. In the past, youth attempted to stand on the shoul-ders of their parents, building on what they built, improv-ing on what they had started. Without this orientation to the past, identity formation is difficult.

Young people are often accused of knowing more clearly what they are against than what they are for; nevertheless, an image of what contemporary youth favor has emerged. In contrast to the fragmented man who has accepted the values related to a technological society, contemporary young people are building their values around the image of "whole" or "complete" man. Their goal is to obtain wholeness within the human community, wholeness within the self, and a wholeness with nature. Youth would have their life-style shaped by this image and the resulting values.

Young people wish to narrow the gap between the haves and the have-nots. Though many youths are affluent, their travels and their exposure to the world via mass media and education have made them ask why a society with know-how cannot close this gap. They would redirect technology to serve all men.

Young people wish to break down the barriers that artificially divide men. Their image of man is "global man." Boundaries such as nationality, race, and religion do not mean much to young people. They seem more aware than adults that the world has changed. In the good Samaritan sense, young people are broadening the boundaries of their concern. They are working toward a new sense of equality, and therefore community, among men.

In keeping with these values, young people are giving peace a high priority. They have seen the futility of a succession of wars. They sense how destructive past attitudes have been. They are trying to "blow the mind" of society at this point, and break out of this destructive pattern. The plaintive cry of their music asks, Why so much sorrow and death within the human community?

Young people are trying to broaden man's concern for his fellowman at two other points. First, not only is an individual responsible in society, but man's institutions are also responsible. Man cannot hide from responsibility within his institutions. Second, these institutions must be concerned with the communities in which they exist. Life cannot be whole if it is conveniently gerrymandered so that institutions can choose where they will be responsible. For example, universities located in or near a ghetto cannot ignore the ghetto just because their students come largely from suburban areas from across the country.

Young people are searching for ways to develop wholeness in the individual as well as in society. They are urging man, instead of narrowly pursuing his own interests, to give himself to a cause beyond himself. If he does this, he will be building human community and finding an integrative element for his life in the process.

Contemporary young people are trying to give man's feelings their rightful place, thereby bringing wholeness. There is an increased interest in all man's senses. Closely related to this is that, instead of being regimented in the service of technology, young people are emphasizing individual freedom.

Finally, young people are attempting to achieve wholeness with nature. In place of the exploitive approach to nature fostered by science and technology, young people are taking a more "friendly" approach. From this rapprochement with nature, young people feel they will restore a dimension to man of which technology had deprived him.

Additional Moods and Feelings

While contemporary youth culture houses many of the moods and feelings of young people, the formation of an identity, learning to be intimate, choosing an occupation, and finding a mate are highly personal tasks. Each youth faces by himself the questions: Who am I? Will I amount to anything? Will my life have meaning? Will I be accepted? Regardless of whether he is associated with contemporary youth culture or not, a youth faces his own personal problems and tasks. He must handle his own unique family background, his own unique potential, and his own unique personal moods and feelings.

A person's ideology and occupation help to form his identity, and when he can find neither, he may be frustrated and unhappy in school. If these are unclear, there is nothing concrete to which he can relate his courses. As a result, he may feel that his courses are irrelevant and that he is wasting his time. An individual's identity forms, as it were, the bottom of a container. When the bottom is in, he feels as if he is "getting something." If the bottom is not in, he may feel as if he is "not getting anything." When a society makes education compulsory or makes it "the thing to do," it makes young people vulnerable to such frustration.

Anger is a common feeling among young people. Anger is aroused in a youth when he senses his well-being is threatened. Nagging restrictions placed upon him by parents or school officials, unjust criticism from parents, teachers or others, trouble with brothers and sisters or with friends, or difficulties in school are frequent irritants that lead to anger.

If a youth feels he can handle the threat, his anger may come out in aggressive behavior. If he is overwhelmed or defeated, or if he fears his anger, it may take a more passive form. Name-calling, belittling others, sarcastic remarks, teasing, and swearing are mild forms of expressing anger. Driving recklessly is a more dangerous form. If a person has low self-esteem, or if expressing anger is taboo, he may resort to indirect or disguised forms of expressing anger such as watching violence, participating in militant organizations, engaging in sexual promiscuity, or engaging in other antisocial acts. In addition, a person may project his anger onto others, making them the target of it.

Depression is another feeling that young people experience. Frequently depression is anger directed against the self. When it is, it means that a youth is not able to handle that anger. If a young person was taught that anger is wrong, his anger may come out in the disguised form of depression. If a person's self-esteem is low, he may direct his anger at himself, and as a consequence, be depressed. Identity diffusion, as well as general confusion over his many problems, may lead to depression. Frequently depression develops when a person senses that time is running out and major problems such as ideology, vocation, and mate selection seem insoluble.

Young people in this stage have their share of anxiety. Though a youth may have rejected the economic and social values of his parents, he may still be influenced by their life-style and values. He is especially vulnerable to anxiety if he is having difficulty in school or with his occupational choice. Rollo May holds that concern over reaching an acceptable level of achievement is the most pervasive cause of anxiety in American society.[66] As a youth approaches the crucial test of whether he will make it successfully into adulthood, he may be the victim of anxiety.

A youth may also experience anxiety over his sexual identity and adequacy. He may fear sexual intimacy and question his readiness for marriage.

Some young people who are not able to handle the problems they face may engage in various forms of antisocial behavior. Stealing is one of the more common forms of antisocial behavior. There is a variety of motivations for stealing. It may be a form of rebellion. It may serve as a way to express anger, a way to get back at parents or other authorities or a way to get back at society. On the other hand, it may be a way to gain status with one's peers, either by possessing something of value, and thereby being the envy of one's peers, or by showing courage and cunning. In still another vein, stealing may be motivated by a need for love and affection. The stolen article may be the replacement for the affection that a youth feels is missing in his own life. Fortunately, most adolescents who steal—often in the form of shoplifting—abandon the practice as they accomplish their tasks and move on to adulthood.

The Defenses of Late Adolescence and Early Adulthood

Faced with the problems of this stage, young people feel the need for defenses. Though they obviously call on defenses that worked for them earlier in life, there are some defenses that are somewhat unique to this stage. These defenses are of two types. First, there are defenses that take group form. Contemporary youth culture serves, among other things, as a group form of defense. While youth culture gives some young people an ideology, it offers others a defense. Indeed the ideological dimension of contemporary youth culture is also a form of defense. Second, there are defenses that individual young people use. Though these are shared by other young people, they do not take group form. We will look at group defenses first and follow with a description of individual defenses.

One of the characteristics of contemporary young people is their noisy criticism of the Establishment. While part of this is related to their ideological position, a large part of it is merely the technique of shifting the focus off themselves onto somebody else. They project their feelings of inadequacy and hesitancy onto their parents. They blame their parents for living a less than meaningful life. Young people also attack society for pursuing the wrong goals. Again, part of this is related to ideology and part is defense. One technique they use is irreverence. They purposely abandon many of the codes of adult society. They commit the "no-noes" of adult society. Such things as the church, patriotism, marriage, civil obedience, accumulation of wealth, cleanliness, proper language, are all flouted. This technique makes adult society look bad, and thereby takes the focus off youth.

Within contemporary youth culture, there is a variety of life-styles. However, a significant number of young people fall into two categories which Simmons and Winograd label "hanging loose" and "tripping out." [67] Those young people who fall into the "hang loose" category cannot accept the current values of American society; therefore they cannot find a place in that society. Because they cannot establish an alternate set of values, they cannot find an occupation, an ideology, and an identity. They become quite immobile. They cannot move ahead. Their technique of hanging loose is a way of avoiding identification with adult society and of trying to buy more time. They are waiting.

Those young people who fall into the category of tripping out have reached the more serious stage of rejecting adulthood, with its accompanying responsibilities. At best, they form a nonadult society of their own, and at worst, they engage in communal escapism. This is a more serious form of defense against an inability to move ahead. On the one hand, there is a mixture of self-indulgence and self-pity in their attitude, and on the other hand, there is self-contempt. They may attempt to capture forever the "swinging" period of adolescence or they may attempt to escape reality altogether by the use of drugs. They are trapped in an all-or-nothing syndrome. Either society must change immediately or they will refuse to join society. At best their approach defends them against a complete loss of integrity. They seem to be poised in a last-ditch stand against a monstrous threat to their weak egos.

Finally, there is another form of defense that is not always recognized as such. This is the defense of involvement. Within contemporary youth culture, there are young people whose ideology has taken shape and whose political and social involvement offers them both a defense against continuing self-doubt and a propellant into the future. Doing volunteer work for political organizations, or joining the Peace Corps, VISTA, or similar organizations sponsored by the church, gives a youth a moratorium for those dimensions of his identity which are still unsettled. At the same time this gives him some practice at being the kind of adult he would like to be. Many young people find this type of defense to be very beneficial. They are able to maintain their personal integrity and yet move in the direction of adulthood.

As we turn now to the individual forms of defense associated with this stage, it is obvious that a youth may use the technique of defending himself by pointing out loudly and clearly what others are doing wrong. Parents come in for a lot of criticism under this procedure. A youth using this technique may give the appearance of certainty and confidence, if not arrogance, when, in fact, he is quite uncertain about himself.

The inability to make an occupational choice, to decide upon a system of values, or to handle some other problems in this stage may bring about a state of apathy in a young person. When he feels as if he is being grasped and held by forces beyond his control, a youth may go into a state of apathy, or even psychic immobility. Apathy is a defense against the problems that a youth is unable to handle. Apathy is a means of forestalling foreclosure.

Some adolescents give the appearance of "not caring." This is a form of defense similar in origin and appearance to apathy. It is often a disguise to cover marked feelings of inadequacy. It may precede the more serious condition of apathy. When the future appears to be too difficult to handle, a youth may enter a state of "not caring" or apathy. He may wish to slow down his life in the face of a future that appears to be rolling in on him.

An early marriage may be a defense. A person may wish to escape an unhappy home. It may also be a means of rejecting or hurting parents. Or it may be a means of establishing independence. Marriage may appear to a young person, particularly a girl, as the solution to her problems. By marrying, a girl may feel that she does not have to make an occupational choice. It may appear to her that, with the decision over a mate settled, she has worked through her adolescent tasks and has entered adulthood. A young person may also enter marriage early to fight against feelings of loneliness, to support a weak ego, or to assure continuing affection. Unfortunately mass media portrays marriage as a cure-all, luring young people into marriage before they are ready for it.

Though the automobile plays many roles, on some occasions it serves young people as a form of defense. A young man may use his automobile to bolster his sexual image. He may use it as a model for the way he would like to appear and the way he would like to be treated. He may take immaculate care of it, spending many hours with it, as a form of sublimation. The automobile may also be a means of working out inner conflicts, through experimentation, testing its capacities, reckless driving, speeding, making noise, etc. It may also serve as a means of getting away from parents and other authorities, and as a private place to talk or make love.

SUMMARY

Many of the moods and feelings of young people in the late adolescent and early adult stage of life are contained in contemporary youth culture. Young people are very much opposed to the fragmentation that exists in our technology-oriented society and they favor values that would bring back wholeness to the individual and to society. A new conception of time has also resulted from our technological and rapidly changing society. As a result, young people have lost their orientation to the past and the future, making it difficult for them to develop their identities.

Besides the moods and feelings that are associated with contemporary youth culture, there are moods and feelings that individuals may have as they face the personal task of identity formation. Young people may experience feelings of frustration, anger, depression, and anxiety. They may also engage in antisocial behavior, such as stealing.

The defenses that young people in this stage use may be associated with contemporary youth culture or may be individual. Young people may criticize others in order to cover their own inadequacies. They may hang loose or trip out because they cannot move ahead into adult society with its values. Others may pursue an ideology that serves as a defense and as a means of helping them move ahead. Individuals may slip into apathy or a state of not caring because they are not ready for adulthood. Early marriage and the automobile may also serve as defense techniques for some young people.

9

PREPARING FOR MARRIAGE

In 1969, the median age of marriage for women was 20.8 and for men was 23.2. Statistics released by the Department of Commerce for that same year indicated that 72.2 percent of the United States population eighteen years of age and older were married. This means that most of the young people of the age for whom this book is written are or soon will be married. It seems appropriate, therefore, to offer some suggestions about how young people may prepare for marriage. I will leave it to someone else to offer suggestions to those young people who choose not to be married how they may prepare for their life in a marriage-dominated society.

The fairy tales with which we have been brought up begin with a description of a young maiden in distress. After a period of hardship, however, she meets Prince Charming. They fall in love, get married, and live happily ever after —at least the story says that they do. That part of the story is not told. The television commercials with which we are growing up follow the same pattern. A young man is in trouble. He may have some nagging ailment, he may be unpopular, or he may use brand X. Someone suggests that he try a specific product. Soon after doing so, he meets a beautiful young lady. They fall in love, are married, and live happily ever after—at least the commercial implies that they do. That part of the story also is not told.

The fact of the matter is, however, that we are not living happily ever after in our marriages. Lederer and Jackson give us a more accurate picture:

> On their wedding day, a young man and a young woman, standing before the priest, minister, or justice of the peace, usually have a high opinion of one another. They over-flow with joyous thoughts. Each has a firm intention of pleasing and nourishing the cherished person who is about to become a partner for life. Some years later, these same two people may be living in a chronic situation of hate, fear and confusion. Each spouse in such a marriage may blame the other and defensively emphasize how hard he tried to be loving, tried to make the marriage a success and tried to keep the other from sabotaging the effort.[68]

The romantic love myth implies that love solves any and all problems; therefore, there is little, if any, need to prepare for marriage. But this myth is leading to marital tragedy! We must make better preparation for marriage than we are presently doing if we hope to have a harmonious and stable marriage.

Marriage and Rapid Social Change

One reason why there is so much instability in marriage is the rapid social change that we are experiencing in our society. Rapid and far-reaching changes in our social order have taken away much of the old support system that marriage once enjoyed, and the new patterns of life that are emerging do not particularly provide stability in marriage nor support the traditional value of marital fidelity. Building and maintaining a marriage in this climate is difficult. A number of factors are involved.

Whereas once, couples lived in the same geographical location as their parents and other relatives, with increased mobility this is no longer the case. The proximity of parents tended to lend stability to a young couple's marriage. The couple generally held the same values as their parents. In addition, the proximity of parents served to circumscribe the amount of conflict that might exist in a marriage. Living at a distance from parents, a couple's values are liable to change, and any conflict that there may be in the marriage may go unchecked.

Increased mobility has introduced individuals to new patterns, life-styles, and values, often markedly different from those with which they grew up. Individuals are exposed to persons of other national backgrounds and religious traditions. There is a greater tendency now than in the past to choose a person with a different background as a marital partner. As a result, spouses bring into marriage conflicting roles, customs, and expectations, all of which make marital stability more difficult to attain.

Another factor promoting instability in marriage is the decline of religious influence in marriage. The stability that a religious interpretation gave to marriage is less available than it once was. Though many couples still have a "religious" wedding, this does not indicate that their marriage will be guided by traditional religious values, rules, and customs.

Closely related to the loss of religious influence in marriage is the increasing acceptance of divorce in our society. There is less of a stigma attached to divorce than before.

Therefore, divorce is a greater possibility.

Still another factor weakening both marriage and family life is the fact that the family has lost many of its earlier functions. In the past, the family was the locus for a variety of activities related to religion, protection, education, and leisure. With urbanization, many of these activities have been delegated to other institutions, leaving the family with fewer functions. With fewer functions to perform, when conflict does come, it is easier than it was before for a couple to break up the marriage.

The fact that the images and roles of both male and female in American society are changing also contributes to instability in marriage. The spouses can no longer rely on stereotyped images and roles to follow or to expect in their partner. This creates one more area where differences may arise and where conflict may develop. For example, the image of "wife" is no longer that of a cloistered, dutiful person whose place is in the home. Now the wife may be educated and wish to pursue a career. This may mean that the husband will have to play a larger role in the tasks that have to be done in and around the home, tasks that he may not wish to do or tasks that he believes belong to his wife.

It should be obvious from these facts that a stable marriage is not easily attained. With more careful preparation young people may be able to develop harmony and stability in their marriage. The rest of the chapter is devoted to suggestions as to how young people may prepare for marriage.

Tasks to Complete Before Marriage

Before he marries, an individual should have much, if not all, of the work of identity formation completed. He should have moved from a state of dependence to independence. He should have gained the ability to be intimate and should have moved from simple aggressive sex to a point where his sex drive is tempered with tenderness. He should have the ability to make *and keep* commitments. He should marry, not merely to have sex, but because he wishes to share his life in companionship with someone.

An individual entering marriage should understand his own needs and, insofar as possible, should know the needs of his partner. The needs that a spouse has often form a hidden agenda to which he gives a great amount of time and energy. In many respects, such needs, more than love, determine the dynamics or pattern of the marriage. For example, a man may have a strong need to achieve in his occupation. As a result, he may give an inordinate amount of time and energy to his work. On the other hand, his wife may have a strong need for reassurance and affection. She may feel that her needs are going unfulfilled, and consequently may accuse her husband of paying too much attention to his job. The role that individual needs play in marriage cannot be underestimated.

One need that many individuals bring to marriage and often is destructive to a marriage grows out of low self-esteem. A person with low self-esteem looks to his marriage, in particular to his spouse, to bolster his weak ego. Much of the attention of such an individual is on himself. His attention and energy are focused on winning arguments, proving himself, defending himself, and attempting to reach perfection. Instead of providing his spouse with the emotional gratification he or she wishes or needs, the person with low self-esteem drains the marriage of emotion. At the same time, he gives the impression to his friends that he is in control, does his share, etc. In his drive for perfection and to cover his insecurity, he expects help from, and places high demands upon, his mate. He expects things to go just right. Both spouses in such a marriage feel cheated and are deeply disappointed.

Often an individual with low self-esteem finds a mate with the same problem. When they were dating, each put up a facade and dated on that basis rather than on the basis of their real selves. Behind this unfortunate game is the fear that the real self would not be attractive enough to win a marriage partner. Each hopes the other will be a strong partner, contributing enough for both. During dating and courtship each makes a show of strength. During early marriage the truth begins to emerge. Frustration, disappointment, resentment, and anger often set in.

It will be helpful if, before marriage, each individual becomes aware of his own needs and the needs of his partner. A couple should talk about such needs. Each partner should examine openly in front of his partner the needs that he wishes his partner to fulfill. By doing this, a couple may determine if an acceptable life-style can be attained; they can also determine whether personality needs may play a disruptive role in their marriage.

Another important area of discussion for couples anticipating marriage is the role that each individual expects to play and the role expectations each has of his partner. There is a tendency for each spouse to play his role as husband or wife and to expect his spouse to play his role as husband or wife on the basis of the roles he observed his mother and father playing. The greater the difference in background of the couple—social, economic, nationality, religion—the greater the potential for misunderstanding, and therefore, the greater the need for discussion of roles and role expectations. For instance, the husband may come from a tradition in which a man did not do any work in the house, while the wife comes from a home where the husband helped with many of the household functions. In marriage, the husband refuses to do household tasks such as dusting, dishes, cooking, and the wife may interpret this as the lack of love or an act of stubbornness directed at her. Or, one spouse may feel that attending church regularly as a family, giving money to the church, and sending the children to church-related schools are all very important values, without which the spouse has deep mental and spiritual agony, while the other spouse is religious but cannot see the importance of these procedures and does not participate. Each partner should bring out into the open before marriage the role he expects to play and the role he expects his partner to play. In this way a couple can work through this potential area of conflict before the relationship is legalized and therefore more difficult to handle.

Young adults anticipating marriage should work on the dynamics of their relationship or the style of their marriage before the marriage is legalized. A struggle for control in early marriage is hazardous. When the relationship is legalized, the complexion of the struggle changes. Each spouse realizes that the relationship is now "for keeps" and tries even harder to see to it that the relationship develops in such a way that his needs and expectations are met. A young couple came for marriage counseling about five months after marriage. Their marriage was one of constant conflict. The wife accused her husband of shirking his duty, of not being able to make up his mind. The husband accused his wife of making all the decisions, of running the marriage, and of undercutting his role as husband. Each had found ways of "getting to" the other. The wife was becoming frigid, while the husband alternated between silence and fits of anger. This couple had become locked in a battle for control over the dynamics of the relationship. Neither partner's needs or expectations were being met. This couple had not discussed before marriage how their marriage would operate. From the first marriage-counseling session, it was apparent that each spouse was struggling to have the marriage operate on his terms. Slowly and painfully they began to understand the problem and work toward its resolution.

There is probably no more helpful ingredient in marriage than clear verbal communication. A couple should establish good habits and patterns of communication before marriage. An individual often expects that his spouse will know what he himself is thinking or feeling. This is especially true when there is a strong element of romance in the relationship. However, the spouse has no way of finding out unless told. For example, a wife has been working hard in the home systematically cleaning each room. At the same time, because of the inclemency of the weather, she has been confined pretty much to the home. She wants very much for her husband to reward her for her efforts and to understand her feelings of confinement. But the husband does not notice her cleaning efforts, nor does he ask her if she would like to go out to dinner. Instead, with a note of self-pity in his voice, he talks about how difficult his job is at present. Each is looking for support and understanding from the other, but neither spouse is rewarded or understood. Disappointment settles in where, if the spouses could have communicated more clearly how they felt, companionship was possible. Little disappointments can easily pile up if they are not handled through clear communication. One of the common problems in early marriage is that one partner feels hurt because his spouse did not understand completely his feelings, wishes, or expectations. To retaliate for this hurt, the spouse sulks, turns off communication, or retaliates more aggressively. It is imperative that a couple develop good communication skills during their dating and courtship years.

The greatest single area of the breakdown of communication in marriage is over information which, though clear to one spouse, is unclear to the other, largely because the individuals come from different cultural or religious backgrounds. Words, gestures, signals, events, are not understood the same way by each spouse. For example, birthdays may be important in the family of one spouse whereas they are hardly noted in the family of the other. A forgotten birthday may be the cause for deep disappointment in a spouse. Where partners come from different backgrounds, a special effort should be made to clarify communication. This process should begin long before marriage.

A couple should attempt to develop a climate of safety in their relationship so that troublesome or conflicting thoughts and feelings can be handled. This calls for maturity in each partner. If a partner feels that he must keep a problem or a feeling to himself because it is too threatening to his partner, the relationship will be crippled. In order to acquire this climate, each individual should be prepared to make himself vulnerable. He must be prepared to show his weaknesses. He must risk having his partner attack. He should be prepared to confess his failures and seek forgiveness and understanding. This attitude will allow his partner to do the same. Pride, competition, and defensiveness get in the way of a deep marital relationship. Individuals often vie for a position of strength and attempt to avoid being vulnerable. But this approach only serves to make the marital relationship shallow. Couples are urged to develop a climate of understanding and forgiveness during courtship days. This will put their marriage on a good footing.

Each individual entering marriage should learn to share his thoughts and feelings with his partner. Having lived with his own thoughts and feelings as an individual for approximately twenty years, he may find it a difficult adjustment suddenly to share his innermost thoughts and feelings with another person. In his family an individual may have learned not to share his thoughts and feelings. Many persons at some time in their life have experienced pain after expressing their thoughts and feelings and have learned to keep these to themselves. We are also the products of our society and learn to show those emotions which society allows. For example, men may show anger but should not cry. In contrast, women may cry but should not show anger.

Individuals tend to carry into marriage those patterns which they learned earlier in life. In doing so, however, they deny themselves the kind of deep companionship possible and desirable in marriage. Individuals also deny their partners the opportunity to share these thoughts and feelings and to provide support where this would be helpful. For example, a person with low self-esteem has held up the facade that he is confident in his job when, as a matter of fact, he is not. He is deeply threatened by some new employees whom the company has hired. Because he has hidden his lack of confidence from his spouse, there is no way in which his spouse can be of help to him in the dilemma. He suffers alone. In contrast, a marriage will be enriched, feelings of isolation in partners will diminish, and partners will feel important to each other if thoughts and feelings of an intimate nature can be shared. Couples are urged to develop this sharing process during courtship so that it is established and working in marriage.

Individuals entering marriage are not always as aware as they might be of the variety of ways in which the male and the female perceive and experience life. It will be very beneficial to a marriage if the partners develop understanding of how life is perceived and experienced by their mates. One area in particular where it will be helpful for the spouses to be aware of these differences is in the area of sex. Obviously the male and female differ in their sex organs. Beyond this—whether it is the result of anatomy, learning, or both—the male and female differ in their thoughts and feelings about sex. For example, the act of sexual intercourse often means something different to the male than it does to the female. As a general rule, what the female wants from sexual intercourse is the feeling that she is loved and will be protected and cared for. In contrast, as a general rule, what the male wants from sexual intercourse is the feeling that he is adequate, admired, and that he has conquered. Therefore, if a husband wishes to make the sex act meaningful and fulfilling for his wife, he will attempt to communicate his feelings of commitment and care to her, and if a wife wishes to make the sex act meaningful and fulfilling for her husband, she will attempt to fulfill her husband's needs.

A second area related to differences between male and female has to do with the pattern of arousal and decline in sexual feelings. As a general rule, the male is aroused more rapidly than the female. Upon ejaculation, the male loses his sex drive. In contrast, the female is aroused more slowly than the male, may have one or more orgasms over a period of time, and then declines in excitement more gradually. In addition, while the sex act would be quite unsatisfying to the male without an orgasm, the sex act may be satisfying to the female without reaching a climax. If husband and wife are aware of these differences, they may be able to fulfill each other's needs more completely and make a good sexual adjustment in marriage.

An area that partners should pursue in discussion is the amount of credence which they will give to romantic love and how much value they will place upon the principle of marital fidelity, i.e., lifelong partnership. There is a potential conflict between these two ideas. Though it is not a new ingredient in marriage, romantic love has come to play a much more prominent and determinative role in marriage than it did in the past. In earlier centuries it was expected that romance would *arise* in a marriage, though individuals often entered marriage for reasons other than romance. More recently, we have come to *choose* a marriage partner on the basis of romance and have held that romance is an important part of marriage. Currently, there is a trend to *terminate a marriage* if romantic feelings for our partner cool or if romantic feelings for someone else develop. *We know that romantic feelings fade.* Therefore, there is a strong possibility that if we place a great deal of credence in romantic feelings, especially following this current trend, we will run into conflict with the principle of lifelong fidelity. The question that young people must decide is whether they will give romantic feelings, or the lack of them, a higher or lower priority than the principle of lifelong partnership.

There is real value in romantic love, in the close and supportive companionship that it can create. Romantic love helps to ease the pain of living in an impersonal society. Perhaps this is why romantic feelings are playing an increasing role. In a mass society, romantic love furnishes an important bond between persons. To be loved does more for the ego than anything else in the world. It means to be appreciated and accepted. Such love, especially when it has matured beyond mere selfish need-fulfillment, can be renewing and creative.

Marital fidelity also has great value. Indeed, marriage contracted on any basis less than a commitment to lifelong partnership will produce something less than is possible where fidelity is present. The love that would develop would be something less than love. Karl Barth describes the result:

> Love would obviously be replaced by what is essentially a constant playing at love, and the full experience and exclusive life-partnership of marriage by a flabby and non-binding experimentation which dispenses with all real discipline and is exempt from that final exertion.[69]

The spouses would always face the haunting question of possible disruption and loss. Instead of producing confidence, it would produce fear; instead of nurturing openness, it would instill hesitancy; instead of producing depth, it would foster shallowness. One of the chief benefits of fidelity is that it urges a couple, instead of looking elsewhere, to look more deeply into each other. There are always dimensions of the other person yet to be discovered, and therefore, more dimensions available in the relationship. For example, a couple who had reached a point of boredom and disappointment, but for whom divorce was not a live option and who, therefore, are determined to do something about their marriage may—perhaps through professional help—discover that there are interests and abilities in each partner that had not been recognized, there is a style of married life that is much more satisfying than the one they had been following, and there is a greater purpose in marriage than the one by which they had been living. In contrast, the spouses who quickly move toward divorce may be on the first leg of an endless search for happiness. With marital fidelity there is the possibility of finding the kind of deep relationship and support that people seek in romantic love. Young people should be aware that romantic feelings may fade, but that there are other ingredients which develop in a good marriage, and that fidelity enables couples to find those ingredients.

The dating process itself may be undermining the traditional value of marital fidelity. In dating, a person inaugurates many relationships, but each relationship is terminated just as quickly if the desired dynamics are missing. This procedure teaches persons how to form and leave relationships. Skills for finding new partners and dissolving relationships are learned well in our dating procedure. Little is learned about fidelity and about how to discover new dimensions in the other person. All of this prepares us better for what is being called "progressive monogamy" rather than for marital fidelity. Real marriage, as opposed to what is fantasied in dating, cannot supply the kind of happiness that romantic fantasies promise. Disillusionment develops easily in a marriage as romance cools. Dating skills of starting and concluding relationship are set in motion almost unconsciously, and spouses continue their seach for marital bliss.

In addition to being in potential conflict with marital fidelity, romantic love has some other characteristics that young people should study carefully. In giving ourselves to the romantic love myth the way we do, we tend to abandon our reason in favor of emotion. The word "love" tends to muddy the water. The word has a sacredness about it, probably because of our Judeo-Christian heritage, which allows it to go unquestioned. In actuality, there is little similarity between the word "love" in the Biblical sense and what we mean by love in the romantic sense. Love in the Biblical sense generally means to have as much, if not more, concern for the other person as you have for yourself. Romantic love is usually more selfish than this. It has to do with whether or not personal emotional needs are being gratified. Nevertheless, if anyone says, "I am in love," nobody dares to question him. Romantic love has been surrounded with an aura of mysticism and mystical power which is not supposed to be questioned.

Another questionable feature of romantic love is that it tends to play down human responsibility. According to the traditional Judeo-Christian understanding, marriages are confirmed in heaven and, therefore, are to be honored with faithfulness. In the romantic love interpretation, marriages are made in heaven or some other ethereal place, and as a result, men are to follow the signals that allegedly emanate from that place. The responsibility for our marriage tends to be placed somewhere beyond ourselves. If our romantic feelings for our partner cool, whether that be our dating partner or our marriage partner, we feel obliged to follow these feelings. We have imputed to these feelings an importance and an authority we dare not deny—or at least which we dare to follow. This conveniently takes the responsibility out of our hands. However, in following this procedure, we fail to take cognizance of the fact that romantic feelings originate within ourselves and should be controlled by us. We are sometimes comical and quite irrational in romantic love. We program ourselves to have romance and then we give romantic feelings unquestioning allegiance. Couples are encouraged to consider the value that they will place on romantic love and on the principle of marital fidelity.

Individuals should have good reasons for getting married. If a couple's marriage is founded on poor reasons, the marriage is liable to be fragile, unsatisfying, and filled with conflict. Counted as poor reasons for marrying are pregnancy, the desire to gain personal independence, marrying because it is the thing to do at a given age, or marrying to get out of a troubled home. The simple drive for sexual expression may propel some individuals into marriage. Parents may feel that they are failures or may feel disgraced if their children are not married by a certain age. The lure of marriage as depicted by mass media may compel youth into marriage before they are ready. Conversely, counted as good reasons for marrying are individual maturity, the ability and desire to care for another, commitment to another, emotional attachment, i.e., romantic love, and the desire to share life's experiences with another. Individuals should consider whether they are ready for marriage, that is, whether they have sufficient maturity, and should sort through as honestly as possible the reasons why they wish to marry.

Finally, it will prove beneficial if a couple moving toward marriage develops a comprehensive philosophy for their marriage. I wish to outline such a philosophy, one that is developed from a Christian perspective.

According to the Bible, the primary purpose of marriage is companionship between husband and wife. In making mankind male and female, God formed a plurality and a polarity so that there might be companionship. The purpose that lay behind this plurality and polarity was the ability for mutual exchange of ideas and feelings, and the ability for mutual support and admiration. Man was created for others. Man's sexuality served the purpose of creating the ability and the need for companionship, and, secondly, as a means of fulfilling the need for companionship. The rule of fidelity was laid down to protect and enrich this concept of companionship.

Having companionship as the purpose of marriage is in contrast to the purpose that the church held for marriage for many centuries: that of procreation. But procreation is an outgrowth of companionship, not the sole purpose of marriage. Procreation is an inadequate purpose for marriage, especially in an era of overpopulation and in an era when medical science has given us many years of married life beyond those normally associated with child rearing. Indeed, part of the current crisis in marriage may be attributed to having procreation as the purpose of marriage. Once their children are launched, many spouses seem to lose their common purpose. They do not have a purpose to undergird their marriage when the children grow up.

After male and female were created, Genesis called them to "be fruitful and multiply, and fill the earth and subdue it; and have dominion over the fish of the sea and over the birds of the air and over every living thing that moves upon the earth." After creating man and woman for companionship and giving them the command to be creative, God saw everything that he had made and pronounced it good. Man and woman *as husband and wife* were established as the caretakers of the earth. First of all, they were to be caretakers of each other. Secondly, their creative endeavors were to be in the form of populating the earth. Thirdly, they were given the entire earth as the sphere of their concern. Our understanding of marriage has often been too narrow; we have not seen this third dimension. Seeing marriage in this larger perspective, a husband and wife will find a comprehensive philosophy that will give their marriage purpose and meaning. And as husband and wife give themselves to procreation and to the betterment of society, they will need the companionship that their marriage offers them.

SUMMARY

Instead of preparing for marriage, we tend to live by the myth that love will bring marital bliss. Unfortunately, the facts are otherwise. Indeed, many marriages in our society are in trouble.

Rapid social change is the major cause behind marital instability. Mobility has brought together individuals from differing backgrounds and has also taken couples beyond the watchful eye of parents and relatives. Religious influence has declined, and with that has come an increase in the acceptance of divorce. The family has lost some of the functions it performed earlier, often leaving a marriage with little purpose. The fact that images and roles of male and female are changing is also contributing to marital instability. In the light of the many factors undermining marital stability, it should be clear that more emphasis should be placed on preparation for marriage.

There are many areas in which individuals and couples anticipating marriage can prepare for marriage. Each partner should attempt to understand his own needs and the needs of his partner; the individuals might well attempt also to understand the role that these needs will play in the marriage. A couple will want to work on the dynamics of their relationship, deciding the style of their marriage, i.e., who has control of what. The couple should also establish a pattern of clear verbal communication before marriage. Each partner will want to learn to share his innermost thoughts and feelings with his partner. A special effort might well be made in the area of communication by partners who come from diverse backgrounds.

A couple will want to develop a climate of safety in their relationship so that troublesome or conflicting thoughts and feelings can be handled. Each individual entering marriage will have to learn to share his thoughts and feelings with his spouse. Individuals should be aware that the male and female differ in their perception and experience of life. One area in particular where male and female differ is in the meaning of the sex act and their sexual response.

A couple should discuss the values they will hold in marriage. In particular, they will want to consider the values of romantic love and marital fidelity and the credence they will give to each. Individuals ought to have good reasons for entering marriage. Finally, a couple should develop a comprehensive philosophy of marriage, one that will sustain their marriage for a lifetime.

CONCLUSION

We have been looking at the developmental stages of adolescence and young adulthood. We have seen the major tasks that the young person must perform and have also seen some of the common problems that young people have during these years. In retrospect we might say that most young people handle adolescence and young adulthood with relative ease. Others, while they may experience a variety of sometimes confusing moods and feelings, and may have to call upon their defenses, also handle this stage of life and move into adulthood. Young people of this age have a reservoir of potential on which to draw, and it is a joy to see them develop their potential. Even those individuals who experience some difficulty with this stage usually have recuperative powers sufficient to assure eventual maturity. They may simply accomplish their tasks a bit more slowly.

The basic task of adolescence and early adulthood is twofold: First, a young person must break away from his parents and develop autonomy. Second, he must develop his own unique identity. Aiding each individual in accomplishing these tasks in moving into adulthood is a life-drive. With this life-drive as a propellant, the adolescent moves through a series of psychosocial assignments, and with the completion of each of these assignments, he moves closer toward adulthood.

The foundation for an individual's personality is already laid by the time he reaches adolescence. Hereditary and environmental factors make up part of that foundation while the other part is determined by the way in which the individual handled the psychosocial tasks of childhood. Though there are these givens and life may seem somewhat determined, the adolescent has a great deal of control over his self. Indeed, one of the more frightening facts that an adolescent faces is that he has his life in his own hands.

Though for purposes of analysis life is broken into stages, the adolescent does not experience his life this way. Life is a process of interrelated events and experiences made up from a combination of homelife, school work and activities, dating, part-time work, and recreational activities. Adolescents grow up in a society in which the values and rules of adult society prevail. Part of their life is influenced by these. At the same time, especially recently, young people have their own subculture with its values and rules. This subculture forms a defense for them from the adult world and also provides them with a place where they learn how to relate to each other, especially to the opposite sex, where they experiment in their imagination and in reality with new ideas and values, and where they grow accustomed to their increased physical and intellectual strength and sexual drives. The identity of the individual adolescent is shaped as he participates in the normal flow of daily activities in which he is engaged with adults and peers.

Breaking away from parents and launching out on his

own is both difficult and essential for a youth. An adolescent often feels guilty over the ideas that he entertains and over the values with which he is experimenting. Yet he knows that he must gain his independence if he is to have self-respect. A youth may feel angry when he finds that life is not black and white the way his parents taught him. He gains a feeling of freedom and autonomy when he finds values and systems which appear as viable or more viable than those held by his parents. While establishing various points of discontinuity with parents is important, establishing points of continuity is equally important, though done less consciously. Often a youth finds the bedrock values that his parents held, values that they were unable to put into practice or establish in society, and attempts to succeed where his parents failed. In this way he finds a place for himself in the world. He is able to establish his autonomy, and yet he is able to identify with his past. Slowly the individual's values come into focus and form an ideology or philosophy of life. They gather from various sources and his identity begins to take shape. He gains self-confidence as he catches a glimpse of who he is.

A youth must feel that he is or will be a contributing member of society. He needs to find a vocation. He cannot be satisfied with just any vocation because a person's vocation is an extension of himself. It must be a vocation that fits his budding self-image. It must express who he is. In his imagination and in reality, a youth "tries on" various vocations, looking for one that seems to fit his emerging self. When he finds a plan or an actual vocation, another dimension of his self falls into place.

The final task of young adulthood is to find a marriage partner. The process of choosing a marriage partner should be carried on with as much care as the process of choosing an occupation, since a marriage partner is also an extension of the self. In addition, couples should prepare for marriage in such a way that the dynamics of the relationship are established to some extent before marriage. It is as important that the dynamics of the relationship fit an individual's self-concept as it is for the partner to fit his identity. When a young adult finds a potential partner and develops an acceptable and workable relationship with that partner, he is ready for marriage and will have established the last dimension of his identity. He has reached and is prepared for adulthood.

NOTES

[1] Erik H. Erikson, "Identity and the Life Cycle," *Psychological Issues,* Vol. 1, No. 1 (1959), p. 52.

[2] Robert E. Nixon, *The Art of Growing,* p. xii.

[3] Erikson, "Identity and the Life Cycle," p. 120.

[4] Arthur J. Jersild, *The Psychology of Adolescence,* 2d ed., p. 61.

[5] Committee on Adolescence, *Normal Adolescence,* p. 884.

[6] Jersild, *op. cit.,* p. 45.

[7] Committee on Adolescence, *op. cit.,* p. 759.

[8] Morris Rosenberg, *Society and the Adolescent Self-Image,* p. 168.

[9] Erik H. Erikson, *Insight and Responsibility,* pp. 115 ff.

[10] Peter Blos, *On Adolescence,* p. 74.

[11] Erikson, *Insight and Responsibility,* p. 111.

[12] *Ibid.,* pp. 126–136.

[13] *Ibid.,* p. 132.

[14] Rollo May, *The Meaning of Anxiety,* pp. 190 f.

[15] *Ibid.,* pp. 12 f.

[16] *Ibid.,* p. 50.

[17] *Ibid.,* pp. 107 f.

[18] *Ibid.,* pp. 128 f.

[19] Jersild, *op. cit.,* p. 381.

[20] Thomas C. Oden, *The Structure of Awareness* (Abingdon Press, 1969), p. 51.

[21] Helen M. Lynd, *On Shame and the Search for Identity* (Harcourt, Brace and Company, 1958), p. 22.

[22] *Ibid.*, p. 207.

[23] Merton P. Strommen, *Profiles of Church Youth* (Concordia Publishing House, 1963), pp. 170–172.

[24] Lynd, *op. cit.*, p. 215.

[25] Blos, *op. cit.*, p. 60.

[26] *Ibid.*, p. 118.

[27] Committee on Adolescence, *op. cit.*, p. 805.

[28] Robert O. Blood and Donald M. Wolf, *Husbands and Wives* (The Free Press of Glencoe, 1960), p. 147.

[29] Harold T. Christensen and Christina F. Gregg, "Changing Sex Norms in America and Scandinavia," *Journal of Marriage and the Family*, Vol. 32, No. 4 (November, 1970), pp. 616–627.

[30] Jersild, *op. cit.*, p. 283.

[31] Edward V. Stein, *The Stranger Inside You*, p. 87.

[32] Lester A. Kirkendall, "Interpersonal Relationships—Crux of the Sexual Renaissance," *Journal of Social Issues*, Vol. 22, No. 2 (April, 1966), p. 46.

[33] Vance Packard, "Possible Elements for a Modern Sex Code," *Pastoral Psychology*, Vol. 21, No. 208 (November, 1970), pp. 33–42.

[34] Erikson, *Insight and Responsibility*, p. 124.

[35] Christensen and Gregg, *loc. cit.*, p. 622.

[36] Lester A. Kirkendall, *Premarital Intercourse and Interpersonal Relationships* (The Julian Press, Inc., 1961), pp. 183–200.

[37] Rosenberg, *op. cit.*, p. 168.

[38] *Ibid.*, p. 52.

[39] Harold W. Bernard, *Adolescent Development in American Culture* (World Book Company, 1957), p. 193.

[40] Jersild, *op. cit.*, p. 237.

[41] Rosenberg, *op. cit.*, p. 112.

[42] *Ibid.*, p. 51.

[43] *Ibid.*, p. 66.

44 *Ibid.,* p. 100.

45 *Ibid.,* p. 105.

46 William James, quoted in R. D. Laing, *The Self and Others* (London: Tavistock Publications, 1961), p. 89.

47 Rosenberg, *op. cit.,* p. 145.

48 Laing, *op. cit.,* p. 174.

49 *Ibid.,* p. 91.

50 *Ibid.,* p. 74.

51 Rosenberg, *op. cit.,* p. 168.

52 Karen Horney, *Neurosis and Human Growth.*

53 Oden, *op. cit.,* p. 135.

54 Rudolph M. Wittenberg, *The Troubled Generation* (Association Press, 1967), p. 84.

55 Kenneth Keniston, *The Uncommitted,* p. 185.

56 Wittenberg, *op. cit.,* p. 86.

57 Gordon W. Allport, *Pattern and Growth in Personality* (Holt, Rinehart and Winston, Inc., 1963), p. 294.

58 *Ibid.,* p. 301.

59 Gordon W. Allport, *The Individual and His Religion,* p. 93.

60 Donald E. Super, "A Theory of Vocational Development," *The American Psychologist,* Vol. 8, No. 5 (May, 1953), p. 186, citing Eli Ginzberg, *et al., Occupational Choice* (Columbia University Press, 1951).

61 Keniston, *op. cit.,* p. 189.

62 Paul Goodman, *Growing Up Absurd,* p. 16.

63 *Ibid.,* p. 41.

64 Keniston, *op. cit.,* pp. 254–255.

65 *Ibid.,* p. 270.

66 May, *op. cit.,* p. 153.

67 J. L. Simmons and Barry Winograd, *It's Happening,* p. 12.

68 William J. Lederer and Don D. Jackson, *The Mirages of Marriage,* pp. 13 ff.

69 Karl Barth, *Church Dogmatics,* Vol. III, Part IV, p. 206.

SUGGESTIONS FOR FURTHER READING

Allport, Gordon W., *The Individual and His Religion.* The Macmillan Company, 1950.

Bailey, Derrick Sherwin, *Sexual Relation in Christian Thought.* Harper & Brothers, 1959.

Barth, Karl, *Church Dogmatics,* Vol. III. Edinburgh: T. & T. Clark, 1958.

Bernard, Jessie, "The Fourth Revolution," *Journal of Social Issues,* Vol. 22, No. 2 (April, 1966).

Blaine, Graham B., *Patience and Fortitude.* Little, Brown and Company, 1960.

———— *Youth and the Hazards of Affluence.* Harper & Row, Publishers, Inc., 1966.

Blos, Peter, *On Adolescence.* The Free Press, 1962.

Brenton, Myron, *The American Male.* Coward-McCann, Inc., 1966.

Christensen, Harold T., and Gregg, Christina F., "Changing Sex Norms in America and Scandinavia," *Journal of Marriage and the Family,* Vol. 32, No. 4 (November, 1970).

Cole, William Graham, *Sex in Christianity and Psychoanalysis.* Oxford University Press, Inc., 1955.

Coleman, James S., *The Adolescent Society.* The Free Press, 1961.

Committee on Adolescence, *Normal Adolescence.* Group for the Advancement of Psychiatry, 1968.

Degler, Carl N., "Revolution Without Ideology," *Daedalus,* Vol. 93, No. 2 (Spring, 1964).

Emerson, James G., Jr., *Divorce, the Church, and Remarriage.* The Westminster Press, 1961.

Erikson, Erik H., *Childhood and Society,* 2d ed. W. W. Norton & Company, Inc., 1963.

——— "Identity and the Life Cycle," *Psychological Issues,* Vol. 1, No. 1 (1959).

——— *Identity: Youth and Crisis.* W. W. Norton & Company, Inc., 1968.

——— *Insight and Responsibility.* W. W. Norton & Company, Inc., 1964.

——— *Young Man Luther.* W. W. Norton & Company, Inc., 1958.

Friedenberg, Edgar Z., *The Vanishing Adolescent.* Beacon Press, Inc., 1959.

Goodman, Paul, *Growing Up Absurd.* Random House, Inc., 1956.

Horney, Karen, *Neurosis and Human Growth.* W. W. Norton & Company, Inc., 1950.

Hunt, Morton, *The Natural History of Love.* Alfred A. Knopf, Inc., 1959.

Jersild, Arthur T., *The Psychology of Adolescence,* 2d ed. The Macmillan Company, 1963.

Josselyn, Irene M., *The Adolescent and His World.* Family Service Association, 1952.

Keniston, Kenneth, *The Uncommitted.* Harcourt, Brace and World, Inc., 1968.

——— *Young Radicals.* Harcourt, Brace and World, Inc., 1968.

Kirkendall, Lester A., "Interpersonal Relationships—Crux of the Sexual Renaissance," *Journal of Social Issues,* Vol. 22, No. 2 (April, 1966).

Lederer, William J., and Jackson, Don D., *The Mirages of Marriage.* W. W. Norton & Company, Inc., 1968.

McCary, James Leslie, *Human Sexuality*. D. Van Nostrand Company, Inc., 1967.

McGinnis, Tom, *Your First Year of Marriage*. Doubleday & Company, Inc., 1967.

May, Rollo, *The Meaning of Anxiety*. The Ronald Press Company, 1950.

Mead, Margaret, *Culture and Commitment*. Natural History Press, 1970.

Muuss, Rolf E., *Theories of Adolescence*. Random House, Inc., 1967.

Nixon, Robert E., *The Art of Growing*. Random House, Inc., 1962.

Noonan, John, *Contraception*. Harvard University Press, 1966.

Oraison, Marc, *The Human Mystery of Sexuality*. Sheed & Ward, Inc., 1967.

Pastoral Psychology, Vol. 21, No. 208 (November, 1970).

Peterson, James A., *Married Love in the Middle Years*. Association Press, 1968.

Reiss, Ira L., "The Sexual Renaissance," *Journal of Social Issues,* Vol. 22, No. 2 (April, 1966).

Rosenberg, Morris, *Society and the Adolescent Self-Image*. Princeton University Press, 1965.

Roszak, Theodore, *The Making of a Counter Culture*. Doubleday & Company, Inc., 1969.

Rougement, Denis de, *Love in the Western World*. Random House, Inc., 1956.

Ruitenbeek, Hendrik M., *The Male Myth*. Dell Publishing Company, Inc., 1967.

Simmons, J. L., and Winograd, Barry, *It's Happening*. Marc-Laird Publications, 1966.

Snyder, Ross, *Young People and Their Culture*. Abingdon Press, 1969.

Stein, Edward V., *The Stranger Inside You*. The Westminster Press, 1965.

Thielicke, Helmut, *The Ethics of Sex.* Harper & Row, Publishers, Inc., 1964.

Wynn, John Charles (ed.), *Sex, Family, and Society.* Association Press, 1966.